ADVANCING THE MISSION

THE ORDER OF DEACON IN THE UNITED METHODIST CHURCH

MARGARET ANN CRAIN

Advancing the Mission: The Order of Deacon in The United Methodist Church

The General Board of Higher Education and Ministry leads and serves The United Methodist Church in the recruitment, preparation, nurture, education, and support of Christian leaders—lay and clergy—for the work of making disciples of Jesus Christ for the transformation of the world. Its vision is that a new generation of Christian leaders will commit boldly to Jesus Christ and be characterized by intellectual excellence, moral integrity, spiritual courage, and holiness of heart and life. The General Board of Higher Education and Ministry of The United Methodist Church serves as an advocate for the intellectual life of the church. The Board's mission embodies the Wesleyan tradition of commitment to the education of laypersons and ordained persons by providing access to higher education for all persons.

Wesley's Foundery Books is named for the abandoned foundery that early followers of John Wesley transformed, which later became the cradle of London's Methodist movement.

Advancing the Mission: The Order of Deacon in The United Methodist Church

Contents

Acknowledgments

This project began with a gracious invitation from Deacon Roger Dowdy to speak to a gathering of United Methodist deacons in September 2019 at Lake Junaluska, North Carolina. As I prepared to speak on *Serving with Holy Boldness,* I was inspired to gather up the threads of narrative that culminated in the United Methodist General Conference decision in 1996 to re–order the ordained ministry of the denomination. I was convinced anew that it was a bold decision inspired by the Holy Spirit, which is rather remarkable for a legislative process that is usually bogged down in parliamentary logjams and divisions. The form of diaconal ministry created by the General Conference in 1996 is the best one I know of in all Christendom. The story of how it came to be is the subject of this book.

Many people were partners in the data collection. At the top of this list is Librarian Daniel Smith and the Styberg Library at Garrett–Evangelical Theological Seminary. When the pandemic allowed Daniel into the library, he searched out documents for me, scanned them, and sent them off. He found some I didn't know I needed. He was a generous and skillful research partner. Others who were especially helpful were Rosalie Bentzinger, Joaquin Garcia, Paul Van Buren, Barbara Garcia, Rena Yocom, Mary Elizabeth Moore, and Linda Marshall. Each of them spent a lot of time with me, answered a lot of questions, and shared historical documents they had kept. Every person I asked for help was ready and willing to give it. Many interviews were conducted over the phone and recorded. Other data came through

Facebook or email interactions. All who are quoted by name in this book have given me their permission. Their names are listed on the following page. Many thanks to each and every one of them.

I also want to thank Deacon Kathy Armistead who helped me envision the scope of this and agreed to publish it. That was very encouraging! Last but definitely not least, I couldn't have done it without the steady support of my partner in life, Jack Seymour, who read multiple drafts; he kept the home fires burning and organized while I plugged away at this. He is a gifted editor and knows how to encourage a writer.

List of People Interviewed for This Book

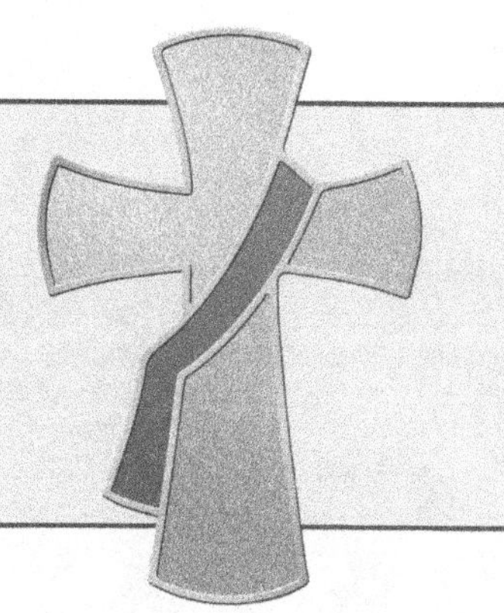

Amy Aspey
Kay C. Barckley
Rosalie J. Bentzinger
Greg B. Bergquist
Richard Lee Buckingham
Shannon Conklin-Miller
Jerome King Del Pino
David Dodge
Diane Wasson Eberhart
Don Ehlers
Charles R. Foster
Deborah B. Fox
Thomas E. Frank
Barbara P. Garcia
Joaquin Garcia
John E. Harnish
Adrienne Ann Ilsemann
Roger Ireson

Robert Kohler
Daniel B. Lee
Sandra W. Lutz
Max Marble
Linda C. Marshall
Patty Meyers
Mary Elizabeth Moore
Susan Sowell Padgett
Tom Rand
Victoria Rebeck
Sharon Rubey
Adrienne Trevathan Stricker
Corinne Sells Van Buren
Paul Van Buren
Anita D. Wood
Rena M. Yocom
Nancy C. Zoller

Prologue
The 1996 Decision

In 1996, the General Conference of The United Methodist Church (UMC) made a bold decision to change its categories of ordained ministry. The order of deacon was recreated in a very different form than had been in existence since the beginning of Methodism in America. Ordained to "Word, order, compassion, and justice[1]," this new deacon was intended to lead the church in its mission to transform the world. Deacons would be partners with elders and laity to strengthen local churches, clarify the mission of the church, and lead and equip the people of God for ministries of witness and transformation.

The decision in 1996 to reorder ministry in the UMC was significant for United Methodists, for the ecumenical church, and for the world. It was significant not because it was a reiteration of the diaconate. That was happening in many expressions of ecumenical Christianity. It was significant because the United Methodist deacon was created to have parity with the elder. This deacon was conceived as "a full and equal order," which was a phrase coined by James Monroe Barnett in 1981.[2] Deacons and elders would be educated together in graduate theological study. Deacons and elders would share full participation in the decision-making structures of the church and in the accountability structures for clergy. No other church made its version of the permanent diaconate so equal. Furthermore, because the deacon and elder were conceived of as distinct, complementary, and equal, the fullness of its mission was reflected in its ordained offices. The United Methodist Church says that its mission is to make disciples of Jesus Christ for the transformation of the world. With elders ordained to Word, service, sacrament, and order; and deacons ordained to Word, service, compassion, and justice, each phrase of the mission is addressed by ordained leaders who focus on church and world. The elder has responded to a call to strengthen the church and nurture disciples. The deacon is called to provide a connection between the nurturing ministries of the congregation and the extension of Christian love, compassion, and justice in its mission to transform the world. With the decision made by the General Conference of 1996, the church was further emboldened to embody its ministry in the world. Two kinds of ordained leaders were set apart to steer the church's mission.

The story of the decision to reorder ministry and its impact is the focus of this book. Beginning in the late 1960s, the founders of the new United Methodist Church (created by the union of The Methodist Church and Evangelical United Brethren) explored how to best serve the needs of the church and its impact on the world. They responded to the social changes of the 1960s: racial and gender equality, the confrontation of the World Council of Churches with sins of the churches in the twentieth century, and the profound shifts in the Roman Catholic Church in Vatican II. The call went out for a more open church that empowered the people of God to make a difference in the world. That call was the beginning of a conversation about how deacons might link the church and the world.

Even before the formation of The United Methodist Church in 1968, some people in predecessor denominations were arguing for including a permanent diaconate in the leadership of the denomination. The impetus had come partly from the ecumenical dialogues that were going on after World War II, which envisioned the deacon leading the church in its *diakonia*, or service, as a meaningful part of the church's ordained leadership. The group of people arguing for the permanent diaconate in the new United Methodist Church was small, but they were convinced that—both theologically and missionally—it made sense.

They never gave up. They continued to advocate, teach, work thru political processes, and listen for God's leading in the midst of it all. Theologically, the diaconate was connected to the ministry of Jesus according to the witness of the Gospel writers. Missionally, it was related to the intense needs of the world. They were particularly touched by the cruelty of the earlier twentieth century: the policies of genocide carried out by the Nazi party, antisemitism in most Western countries, the destruction wrought by the war in Europe, and the shocking detonation of atomic bombs in Japan. The United States was watching bread lines of bedraggled, weary people and becoming aware of the ugly racism that included the barbarism of lynching and burning crosses that generated fear in the hearts of oppressed people of color.

Rosalie Bentzinger, who led The United Methodist Church's diaconate (1979–1994), wrote,

> As World War II drew to a close, a group of clergymen in cell block 26 of Dachau Concentration Camp began to secretly discuss, at considerable risk to themselves, some ways to revitalize the church in the wake of the devastating war. These discussions led to Wilhelm Schamoni's published works on a restoration of the diaconate as a permanent order. Implications of his writing were discussed in "diaconal circles" which were formed in parts of Germany. German theologian Karl Rahner became involved, heavily influencing the bishops at Vatican II, and the permanent diaconate with a focus on service to the world became a reality in the Roman Catholic Church. (1991, 1)

After the war ended, the Christian church had to take stock of its role in allowing and sometimes supporting those atrocities perpetrated by the Nazis. Much of Western Christianity had failed to see or stop the murder of more than six million Jews, gypsies, and homosexuals by the white supremacist Nazis. In addition, Europe was devastated by bomb damage and economic crisis. So many people with so many urgent needs! How could the church respond? In the United States, civil rights issues were erupting, and many Protestants, both Black and White, were seeking change. Perhaps the church needed leaders who were focused on the needs of the world and would lead the church's mission to the vulnerable and oppressed. Vatican II led the way, but Protestants were responding as well.

In 1968, The United Methodist Church was birthed from the merger of two denominations: The Methodist Church and the Evangelical United Brethren. One word was saved from the old title of each: *United* and *Methodist*. The new denomination rested on the assumption that a system of agencies could resource and lead the church in its ministries, while bishops would appoint pastors for all its congregations. These congregations were seen as mission outposts. Like the predecessor denominations, the UMC was designed as a representative democracy, roughly parallel to the government of the United States, with the General Conference as the primary legislative component of the institution, the only group that can speak for the church.

What drew the Evangelical United Brethren and The Methodist Church together was a common heritage from John and Charles Wesley, a heritage that was both theological and social. The Wesley brothers were ordained in the Church of England, educated at Oxford, and steeped in the liturgical practices of that tradition. But they were also frustrated with the lack of spiritual energy or passion they saw in the church. They were hungry for a spiritual renewal. And they saw the need to preach and teach their method to people who were struggling both spiritually and physically. John Wesley began to preach in fields and organize classes and bands. People responded, and the movement grew. The Wesleyan revival spanned the mid- to late-eighteenth century, the same time that colonists were moving to the North American continent and steadily creating farms and towns. This heritage of traditional liturgical worship and spiritual growth combined with an alertness to the real needs of people in their daily lives was transported to the new world by enthusiastic believers in the Methodist revival. When the American colonies became independent of their British rule, American Methodists needed to leave the Church of England and make their own church where the Word could be preached and the sacraments duly administered. John Wesley ordained Francis Asbury and sent him off to America. The rest is history.

John Wesley's dual focus on spiritual formation and social reformation was a part of the new American movement from the beginning but was marred by racism from the start. Before long, Black Methodists began to leave the denomination and form their own. The African Methodist Episcopal and the African Methodist Episcopal Zion Churches were started due to the inequities experienced by Black church goers early in the development of the denomination. Early in the nineteenth century, new struggles developed in the original Methodist Church when some Methodists began to argue that slavery was incompatible with Christian faith. A split over that issue created The Methodist Episcopal Church and The Methodist Episcopal Church South. The northern church believed that slavery was theologically and socially indefensible and demanded that it come to an end. The southern church argued that their culture and rights were being attacked. So, they divided. Those entities came back together in 1939 as the Methodist Church. That merger included structural racial segregation; the northern church agreed to a nongeographical jurisdiction, laid over the five geographical jurisdictions in the United States. The nongeographical Central Jurisdiction would be made up of Black congregations and clergy. African American Methodists were sacrificed for the sake of "unity."

The denomination had remained overwhelmingly White when racist practices forced people of color to leave and form the African Methodist Episcopal Church and the African Methodist Episcopal Zion Church in the late eighteenth and early nineteenth centuries. Yet, the denomination repeatedly experienced movements seeking to broaden representation at every level and in every office. When the merger occurred in 1968, dismantling the racially segregated jurisdiction that had been built into the structure of the Methodist Church in 1939 was part of the agreement. The merger of 1939 had also included the Methodist Protestant Church that had never had an episcopal system. The Methodist Protestants pushed for a broader role for laity in the governing of the church. That practice would be a factor in the growing understanding that all Christians are called to ministry. Finally, the denomination was recognizing that God could call and equip diverse people to lead the church!

During the nineteenth century, women pushed for suffrage in the political processes of the United States and for suffrage in both the northern and southern branches of the church as well. Justice and inclusion were continually discussed and debated. Eventually, the governing bodies of the church came to include laypersons as well as clergy, women as well as men, and persons of color as well as White persons. In 1956, full clergy rights were made available to women. By 1968, denominational seminaries enrolled more women students, and they were being approved for ordination and full conference membership in annual conferences. Every one of these justice moves was resisted and hard fought. The church that claims to be focused on social and personal holiness has always had a lot to learn about who God loves.

A Permanent Diaconate Emerges in The United Methodist Church

If you are reading this book, you likely already know this history. The focus of this project will be the General Conference decision of 1996, which reordered ordained ministry for The United Methodist Church. Between the formation of The United Methodist Church in 1968 and the action of the 1996 General Conference, the UMC studied and discussed and debated how to organize its leadership, both lay and ordained.

Particularly at issue was diakonia. The UMC dialogue echoed a larger dialogue in Christianity that sought to revive the deacon as an office distinctive from that of the presbyter or elder. Vatican II had proposed a permanent diaconate in 1963. The World Council of Churches' document *Baptism, Eucharist, Ministry* (1982) had recommended a threefold pattern of bishop, presbyter, and deacon. The United Methodist Church's expression of diakonia evolved during those decades: at first it was a consecrated lay worker in 1968, then diaconal ministers in 1976, and finally ordained deacons were established in 1996.

This book will attempt to construct a narrative about this evolution and the key players in it. The story of the political and theological developments that led to the 1996 decision will reveal how the idea grew, who were the leaders who kept the idea alive, and how it was finally approved. This is *not* the only conflict that the UMC struggled with during those decades, but perhaps this narrative will help to illuminate some of the others. The church always struggles over which missional needs take precedence and who should lead the church. And competing theologies are always present. Issues related to mission, leadership, and theology are part of this history.

The decision of 1996, I will argue, was a very good one, but it ignited another dialogue about the meaning of ordination and its connection to the sacraments and itineracy. The deacon is ordained but not authorized to preside at the sacraments. This prohibition is troublesome because ordination and the sacraments have been linked throughout Christian history. In addition, deacons do not itinerate in the same manner as elders. Because the ordained elder itinerates in service to the missional needs of congregations, and ordained deacons find their places of service in a process more akin to a call system, some continue to question the validity of ordination for the deacon. For some Methodists, itineracy is inextricably tied to ordination. As this manuscript is completed, the report from the Commission for the 2016–2020 Study of Ministry Commission has been submitted for General Conference action and may fire up the dialogue over these issues yet again.

The ordained deacon is not the first break with tradition, however. When Wesley ordained Francis Asbury and sent him to organize and order the church in the new United States, he was not a bishop and, therefore, was not authorized to ordain. Wesley broke with tradition because of the needs of the Methodists in the newly independent nation. Before the revolution, the Methodist movement depended on the Church of England to provide the sacraments through regular eucharistic services conducted by clergy who were duly ordained by bishops in the apostolic tradition. But without the Church of England and its clergy present in the independent country, Wesley had to act outside that tradition. I imagine how he must have struggled with the decision, but he ordained Francis Asbury and sent him off to start a new church. Asbury made himself superintendent (bishop) and ordained others for this mission. He sent them out to ride circuits where they found people ready to be baptized and to hear them preach. Their circuit ministry eventually formed congregations and "churches" across the frontier—thousands of them. And these congregations identified leaders who could teach and pray and lead singing, along with other leaders who could care for the sick and feed people who were hungry. Personal and social holiness were part of the ethos of this denomination from the beginning.

The Diaconate Is Linked to the Push for Full Participation of Women

Another tradition that needed to be revised concerned the roles of women. By the twentieth century, the Methodist Episcopal Church and Methodist Episcopal Church South had become very large and very ordered institutions. They each had agencies such as a Board of Education, a hymnal and *Book of Worship*, and a book of law called the *Discipline*. Every four years, the elected lay and clergy representatives would go to a General Conference where the *Discipline* could be revised. Those voting were exclusively men until the late nineteenth century. Ordination was an office for men only. In 1956, General Conference approved ordination and full conference membership for women in The Methodist Church; in 1980, the first clergywoman was elected as a bishop of the church.

For many centuries, Western Christianity had been deeply enmeshed in the patriarchal cultural practices of Western Europe. The Roman Catholic Church ordained only men. Women who were called to ministry were often confined to cloistered communities. The Protestant Reformation did little to change those practices. This began to break up in the nineteenth century with the establishment of deaconess communities in urban settings. Laywomen in settlement houses taught English to immigrants, cared for the sick, and helped some of the most vulnerable in the city to find their way. The Methodist Church General Conference officially approved the office of deaconess in 1888. Deaconesses were expected to remain single; when they married, they left the community. At that same General Conference, five laywomen who had been elected as representatives by their annual conference in Illinois were seated as delegates with voice and vote, but they were later replaced by men. The sexism had been challenged but not conquered.

Some women had always been effective preachers and teachers, but they were the exception. Ordination with full clergy rights had never been part of the bargain. Wesley's movement in England had relied on lay leadership for the small groups that were essential to "the method" that led to spiritual growth. He included women as class leaders and in other roles. That practice continued in the colonies as methodism spread, but there were clear limits for women.

The Diaconate Is Linked to the Meaning of Ordination

For many centuries, ordination was assumed to be to leadership *in* the church, although exceptions were made for chaplains, professors, and so on. For some time now, the *Book of Discipline* (or *Discipline*) has included the description that "ordination is God's gift to the church." The 1984 *Discipline* ¶110 states, "The ordained ministers are called to specialized ministries of Word, Sacrament, and order." Ordination was focused on what happened *in* the congregation. Yet, from the beginning, the Methodist movement has had a dual focus of spiritual formation and social reformation. Ordination authorized those who cared for the ecclesiastical things; the work of social holiness was left to laypersons. In a way, it was the *trickle-down* notion of how to reform the systems of the world with their oppressions and disregard for human flourishing. As long as laypersons heard a good sermon and received the means of grace in good order, they could be left to care for social reformation.

The General Conference of 1996 initiated a break with that tradition when they approved an office of ordained deacon whose ministry was to focus on Word, service, compassion, and justice. The language they approved for the *Discipline* was, "Those who respond to God's call to lead in service and to equip others for this ministry through teaching, proclamation, and worship and who assist elders in the administration of the sacraments are ordained deacons" (*Discipline* 1996, ¶303.2). By 2016, the description was more concrete as it named the focus of the service of deacons: "Those who respond to God's call to lead in service, word, compassion, and justice and equip others for this ministry through teaching, proclamation and worship and who assist elders in the administration of the sacraments are ordained as deacons" (*Discipline* 2016, ¶303.2). This language more clearly differentiated deacons from elders "whose leadership in service includes preaching and teaching the Word of God, administration of the sacraments, ordering the Church for its mission and service, and administration of the *Discipline* of the Church" (¶303.2).

Why Does This Matter?

This book is an attempt to record the narrative of how this decision came to be and why this story needs to be told. I contend that the United Methodist version of the diaconate, the ordained deacon, is the most fully conceptualized in Western Christendom. Other churches—Episcopal, Roman Catholic, Lutheran, British Methodist—that have an ordained deacon have not genuinely embraced the deacon as parallel to the elder or presbyter. Instead, the deacon is somehow *less than*. An image that captures this for me is that of the nesting dolls such as the ones from Russia, Poland, or Estonia that tourists still marvel at and bring back home from their travels. If the little doll at the center or heart of the nest is the layperson who is baptized, then the next doll that covers it is the deacon. The larger one covering the deacon is the elder or presbyter, and the largest, which encapsulates or holds all the others, is the bishop. To look at it as you dismantle the doll, the one that first presents itself is the bishop. Inside that bishop is the elder. Inside the elder is a deacon, and inside the deacon is the baptized Christian. The decision of the 1996 General Conference is remarkable because it eliminated the nesting ministries by eliminating sequenced ordination and expanded the decision of 1976 that made ministry the work of all Christians.

Depending on the order to which you are called, you are ordained as an elder or a deacon: one permanent ordination to a specific form of ministry. The elder is ordained to Word, service, sacrament, and order. The deacon is ordained to Word, service, compassion, and justice. The Christian denominations that have maintained two-step ordination for their presbyters have (perhaps inadvertently) kept deacons in a lower position in the leadership of the church privileging sacramental administration over the embodied work in the world.

Our Methodist heritage already contained a concept of elder with a single ordination. The Evangelical United Brethren practice was that an elder was ordained only once. The duties changed with the appointment. Elders itinerated and might be appointed as pastor of a congregation, as an administrator for a district, or even as superintendent of a conference for a term, but always remained an elder. However, in the debate leading to the elimination of sequential ordinations for elders and a permanent deacon in full connection, that part of our history was forgotten.

The United Methodist deacon of today is required to have completed academic work at the graduate level in theological studies, parallel to the requirements for ordination as an elder. Other denominations usually educate their deacons, deaconesses, and diaconal ministers in diocesan educational programs. These are often not as rigorous as the graduate-level courses that United Methodist deacons complete. Because those seeking ordination as United Methodist deacons are educated alongside those who seek ordination as elders, their parity is generally accepted by those who are more recently ordained. The day is coming soon when deacons will no longer hear their elder colleagues say, "I am a deacon too." Those older elders who were ordained as transitional deacons before 1996 seem to have a difficult time understanding the unique call and identity of deacons. Newer elders who were ordained only once are more comfortable with the distinctiveness and parity of their deacon colleagues.

The 1996 General Conference approved this reordering of ministry after several quadrennia of attempts to create an official theology of ministry and practice that would be consistent with that theology. It retained the language that ordination "is a gift from God to the church" (*Discipline* 1996, ¶303). And it affirmed that God calls leaders to be set apart for both the gathered church and ministry in the world. Paragraph 319 describes deacons as those who "fulfill servant ministry in the world and lead the Church in relating the gathered life of Christians to their ministries in the world, interrelating worship in the gathered community with service to God in the world." This connection of church and world is expressed in the powerful words of ¶107: "The people of God, who are the church made visible in the world, must convince the world of the reality of the gospel or leave it unconvinced." Four years later, the 2000 General Conference added ¶120: "The mission of the church is to make disciples of Jesus Christ." Then in 2004, the General Conference added more to the sentence: "The mission of the church is to make disciples of Jesus Christ by proclaiming the good news of God's grace and by exemplifying Jesus' command to love God and neighbor, thus seeking the fulfillment of

God's reign and realm in the world" (*Discipline* 2004, ¶121). This version is perhaps the strongest description of the Church's dual mission to church and world and supports the need for two forms of ordained leaders. In 2008, the phrase "for the transformation of the world" was added, and it remains.

The 2016–2020 quadrennium Commission for the Study of Ministry produced a document released in early 2020. The Commission was tasked with creating a theology of ordination. All of us who have observed The United Methodist Church over the years recognize that trying to write theology in a meeting with a thousand voters using Roberts Rules of Order is impossible. Paragraphs written by committee are often jumbled and contain contradictions. Famously, Walter Muelder said in 1968 that theological work cannot be done on the floor of General Conference, and no one since has disagreed. Nearly every General Conference has authorized a Commission to study ministry and asked it to clarify the theology of ordination. Nevertheless, the denomination continues to operate with a theology that connects ordination with sacrament and contradictory practices that separate ordination and sacrament. We have ordained clergy who are not authorized for administration of the sacraments (deacons) and appoint laity who are authorized to administer the sacraments (local pastors). Because the 2020 General Conference had to be postponed due to a pandemic, that theological statement will not be acted upon or received until at least 2022, but it clearly reflects the broad understanding that mission needs ordained leadership: "an embodied posture of service and an enfleshed participation in the sublime movement of Spirit—in pursuit of a transformed world" (ADCA 2020, 1005).

I invite you, dear reader, into the narrative of The United Methodist Church's decisions to have two kinds of ordained leaders: one focused on ordering the sacramental and worship life of the congregation, and one focused on leading the work of transforming the world into a place of compassion and justice. These leaders are the enfleshed mission. Deacons, elders, and laity join together in the mission of The United Methodist Church: "to make disciples of Jesus Christ for the transformation of the world." The narrative is chronological, because the history of the UMC occurs in four-year chunks; each General Conference brings the possibility of change. Sometimes, the changes are incremental; sometimes change is lightning fast. Most General Conferences include some returning delegates who were influenced by the proposals and debates from four years ago. Some of the narrative needs to be told in four-year chunks; some chapters cover a longer period of time. But always, this story should return to the ultimate goal of raising up leaders for the church's efforts to contribute to the fullness of the reign of God. We pray, "Thy will be done on earth as it is in heaven." That is the goal of the diaconate.

Many people have contributed to this book who were active participants in this history. I have interviewed them and have their permission to use their descriptions of what happened. A full list of people I interviewed may be found in the chart following the acknowledgments page. Most began with a phone interview which I recorded and then transcribed. However, many continued through email and social media. Truly, this was a collaborative effort!

1 First Steps on the Path to a Renewed Diaconate

1968: A New Denomination Is Born

1968 was a tumultuous year in the United States. Its people were deeply divided over the war in Vietnam. University students were protesting. Dr. Martin Luther King Jr. was assassinated in April, setting off demonstrations and igniting desperation. Conversations about the role of women in culture were happening around dinner tables, and women were beginning, once again, to demand their rights. Meanwhile, the Uniting Conference that formed The United Methodist Church met in May in Dallas. Its goals were idealistic; this joining of The Methodist Church and the Evangelical United Brethren would reunite two portions of the fractured branch of Protestantism birthed by John and Charles Wesley and their revival movement. The church's hope for unity and harmony was in stark contrast to the turmoil in American culture.

The traditions and structure of two denominations had to be merged. The Methodist Church developed from an informal frontier gathering under the leadership of Francis Asbury in 1784. However, before many years had passed, it suffered division over racial discrimination, slavery, and the role of laity. By the second half of the nineteenth century, both the northern and southern churches had become large denominations with published Sunday school curricula, a hymnal, liturgies, educated preachers, hospitals, colleges, universities, campgrounds, parsonages, and church buildings in every county and at many crossroads of the United States. By the mid-twentieth century, The Methodist Church had become a multilayered institution with more than ten million members. It had offices at the national level with influential staff such as the Board of Education and the Board of Pensions. It sent missionaries around the globe. But it also had a jurisdiction designed to keep people of color separate from the predominantly White churches. The Evangelical United Brethren (EUB) was much smaller and slightly less hierarchically organized, but it too was Wesleyan in theology and valued an educated clergy. The EUB also had national boards to teach, provide resources for the denomination, uphold standards, and deploy missionaries.

The Methodist Church had been formed by the merger of three bodies in 1939: the Methodist Episcopal Church, the Methodist Episcopal Church South, and the Methodist Protestant Church. Part of the compromise that made this union possible was that most of the African American congregations would be segregated into what was euphemistically called the Central Jurisdiction. These widely separated congregations could share their pastors and bishops only among themselves, thus effectively preventing racial mixing in the churches. The African Americans who were part of the 1939 decision did not support it, but they were outvoted. The Methodist Church structure ensured that it would remain racially segregated.

The Evangelical United Brethren Church, which emphasized holiness, was also the result of a merger. In 1946, the Evangelical Church and the Church of the United Brethren in Christ came together. They shared a Wesleyan heritage and German cultural roots. Both churches had begun in the early years of the United States, and both groups were anti-slavery. Their bishops were elected for four years. They also started a number of colleges and two seminaries.

As we trace the steps leading to the decision of 1996 to create a permanent ordained order of deacons, one difference between the denominations in the 1968 merger is significant. The Methodist Church practiced two-step, sequential ordination for its clergy: elders (presbyters) were first ordained as deacons with probationary membership in the annual conference where they remained "on trial" until they were ordained as elders with full membership in the annual conference. The Evangelical United Brethren ordained once and admitted the newly ordained as members of the annual conference; its elders were never ordained as deacons. The EUB did not elect bishops for life, but the Methodists did. In other ways, both structurally and theologically, they were similar. Both denominations had bishops with the power to move and appoint clergy to serve wherever they were needed within the annual conference. Both denominations certified and commissioned people with training and skills in specialized ministries such as Christian Education and music. Both had sprung from the Wesleyan renewal movement and shared an understanding of grace as well as the need for spiritual formation alongside social action. So, where there were many similarities, there also were some significant differences that had to be negotiated and resolved, especially racial segregation. The new denomination gave itself four years (a quadrennium) to sort all that out and came to the General Conference of 1972 with a plan for the structure and national boards they needed.

The Tumultuous 1960s in the United States

The new denomination and its ordering of leadership did not happen in a vacuum; 1968 was a tumultuous year. The Uniting Conference for the church took place April 21–May 4, 1968 in Dallas, Texas. Dr. Martin Luther King Jr. had been assassinated April 4th. Senator Robert Kennedy would be assassinated in June. The Democratic convention in Chicago later that summer would come unglued with police and demonstrators clashing in the streets. Americans were preparing to orbit the moon. Too many Americans were dying in Vietnam, and the nightly news showed body bags with American soldiers who had been killed in the fierce Tet offensive. Tensions were high, and opinions were deeply divided about the direction the country should take.

Keller, Moede, and Moore, authors of *Called to Serve*, a book about the diaconate published by the General Board of Higher Education and Ministry in 1987, identify five cultural forces that contributed to the turmoil. The first is *recurring emphases on partnership and participation* (49). Business, government, art, and the church all experienced this call for more grassroots power. Even the work of research began tentative movement toward acceptance of qualitative research methodologies and careful listening as ways to collect data where only statistics had been thought useful to describe reality. The 1968 *Book of Discipline* defines the church as "the people of God" in ¶301: "All Christians are called to ministry, and theirs is a ministry of the people of God within the community of faith and in the world." This was a departure from the earlier understanding that ministry was the work of clergy. Liberation theologies were attending to the experience of people at the grassroots; these new theological methods and their insights were gaining a foothold in the church. A groundswell of excitement about the promise of partnership and responsibility at the grassroots was present in many parts of the culture.

Related to the idea of partnership and grassroots power was the *emerging women's consciousness about the marginalization of traditional women's vocations including certain church vocations* (Keller 1987, 49). More and more women were seeking to be full partners in governance and professions. They also wanted to share power. Feminist theologians were publishing fresh biblical interpretations, and gender studies were proliferating in universities and theological schools. Women were questioning many assumptions about what they could and could not do. I recall a conversation around the dinner table at the home of my parents. I was a graduate student at the time, and I was shocked to hear my father resisting the idea that women needed liberation from their confining gender roles of mother and homemaker. We argued, but neither of us changed our mind. Despite my conviction that women needed liberating, I was not acting to live into my own options. That year, I decided to drop out of the PhD program because I was going to be "over-educated to be a faculty wife." When I shared that decision with my faculty advisors, no one argued with my logic. While liberation seemed right to me, I had no idea of how I might embrace it for myself.

In the church, women were entering theological schools in increasing numbers. They were also being ordained and seeking appointments. The United Methodist Church was stressed as it adjusted to the challenge of appointing women to congregations that resisted having a woman as their pastor, and bishops also were trying to figure out how to appoint clergy couples. Competing values about the changing roles of men and women were swirling around all of us in 1968.

A third cultural dynamic in the 1960s and 1970s was *heightened awareness of ethical issues in the public realm* (Keller 1987, 49). The Moral Majority became part of the political scene, and its values were hotly debated. Liberation theologies from Latin American and Black scholars made the church aware of inequalities and oppressions both at home and around the world. A presenting issue in 1968 was the war in Vietnam but, because it was primarily fought by soldiers from marginalized communities and people of color who could not avoid the draft, the war raised to public consciousness the racism and sexism embedded in the US culture.

The public schools of the United States were slowly desegregating. The Brown vs Board of Education Supreme Court decision in 1954 had decreed that racial segregation must end; the practice of "separate but equal" was inherently unequal and schools must integrate. This set off resistance of all sorts. Many new private schools were started, and White families sent their children there. Other areas openly resisted; eventually, the national guard had to be called in to enforce integration in many communities. In the northern states, *de facto* segregation was the result of neighborhoods that were informally segregated by real estate, banking, and governmental practices. Busing was not welcomed by either the Black neighborhoods or the White community, but it seemed to be the only solution. The struggles and resistance to desegregation went on for decades. The Methodist Church was segregated too, but more and more of its leaders were calling for an end to such practices. Dollars were set aside to assist the Ethnic Minority Local Churches. When voices from the grassroots gained a hearing, the oppressions were named. Both church and society sought to address them.

A fourth dynamic identified by Keller, Moede, and Moore is *a search for roots* (1987, 50). In public schools, the curriculum stressed a return to fundamentals. The churches looked to the Bible and especially the New Testament as a model for their organization. Renewed biblical scholarship by feminist theologians searched for answers to questions about women in biblical cultures, seeking to separate truth from dated cultural values, to understand the multiple roles men and women had played throughout the life of the church. Laity were encouraged to engage in Bible study too and access the new scholarship.

Ecumenical dialogues sent liturgists back to the practices of the early church as it developed a sacramental theology. Documents from the early church such as the epistles and Acts were scoured for answers to questions about how to identify those who were called and equipped to be set apart as leaders. Studies of Acts 6 seemed to offer one answer to questions about how to set apart leaders for the church. Those supporting renewal of the diaconate particularly searched for roots to claim a space in the twentieth century. This search revealed that the deacon was an established office in the hierarchy of the church in the early centuries of Christianity, closely connected to and often succeeding the bishop he had assisted.

The fifth cultural dynamic named by Keller, Moede, and Moore (1987, 50) is the *changing patterns of leadership*, which in the twentieth-century church translated to a growing reliance on professionals to do much of the organizing and ministry. This trend had begun early in the century. According to Dorothy Jean Furnish (1976, 23–24), the new profession of religious education promised to improve the Sunday school—which had been a lay movement—and thereby improve the moral health of the nation's youth: "The academic foundations for this new profession would be two: (1) the best of pedagogy as expounded primarily by John Dewey, and (2) the best of biblical scholarship." Seminaries hired professors of religious education, and associations were formed during this optimistic period. After 1930, the depression drained the air from the balloon and few churches could support a professional director of religious education. This would surface again prior to the merger of 1968.

The academic field of religious education and the ministry profession were on the rise again following World War II. Of course, women were joining the workforce in large numbers, and the cadre of volunteers to keep the church going was shrinking. However, the drive for excellence also meant that many congregations were paying musicians, nursery workers, educators, and youth workers to lead those ministries. The denomination defined standards for certifying workers' skills.[1] These movements toward professionalization did not come without controversy, of course. How does the small congregation afford to pay a professional to lead youth? What is just compensation? How can these professionals obtain pension funds? Who evaluates their effectiveness? At the heart of these changing patterns of leadership were questions about power: Where does the power reside? Is good leadership empowering?

Despite the unrest and disorder of the larger cultural scene, hopes for the new denomination were high in 1968. This merger would end the racial segregation that had been in place for decades in The Methodist Church. It would make the ten-million-member Methodist Church even larger with the addition of the members of the Evangelical United Brethren. It would spread scriptural holiness across the land![2]

Specialized Ministries and Professional Certification

The new denomination came out of a tradition that had embraced the Sunday school movement of the late-nineteenth and early-twentieth century. The publishing house was creating books and printed curriculum for learners of all ages. The curriculum maintained high standards for its pedagogy and biblical scholarship. Institutions of higher education offered degrees to those who were to take their place in the educational ministries of the church. In addition, both denominations had established standards by which persons could be certified as director or minister of Christian education. The 1948 General Conference of The Methodist Church approved a plan for certification of directors of Christian education, so it was well established before the 1968 merger. In order to achieve this professional certification, one needed to have both a bachelors and graduate degree in Christian Education or Divinity. These standards appear in the 1964 *Book of Discipline* of The Methodist Church and continue in the 1968 *Book of Discipline* of the new United Methodist Church. The General Board of Education administered the professional certification standards for Christian education. You could be certified as a *minister* of Christian education if you were ordained. The *director* title designated laypeople with a graduate degree in Christian Education. Educational assistants were others working in the field of Christian education but lacking graduate level higher education. Certification for music ministry followed the same patterns. People who had met the standards were recognized at annual conference and listed in the conference journal.

The Evangelical United Brethren 1967 *Discipline* also mentions the director of Christian education as a recognized position within the denomination. The Department of Ministry in the Division of Higher Education of the national Board of Education was responsible for both a course of study and administration of testing for people who chose that field of service (¶1379). This director of Christian education was named in the same paragraph with candidates for ordained ministry. The responsibility for certification resided in the annual conference. Professors of Christian education from the two denominational seminaries were required members of the Board of Education. Clearly, the specialized educator was valued and credentialed in the denomination. The Evangelical United Brethren Church also had a set of standards for certification for professional Christian educators, which were administered by annual conferences. When the two denominations merged, they agreed on a common standard and continued certification.

In 1965, Corinne Sells, for example, (who later became an ordained deacon) met the standards as administered by the Methodist General Board of Education for certification as a director of Christian education. She received this recognition at the West Wisconsin Annual Conference where she had taken a position at First Methodist Church in Madison. Her certificate reads:

> This is to certify that Corinne Elizabeth Sells has met the standards of the General Board of Education for Directors of Christian Education, as provided in the Discipline of The Methodist Church, and is privileged to assume the title of a certified Director of Christian Education in The Methodist Church, subject to annual review of this certification. Signed on behalf of the Board of Education of The West Wisconsin Annual Conference, North Central Jurisdiction, of The Methodist Church.

The service included a series of questions. The first one asks the person to affirm that she or he is called to this work: "Do you believe in your heart that you have been led by the Spirit of God to assume the responsibilities of the office in which you are to be consecrated?" Other questions ask the candidate to be diligent in prayer, be loyal to the church, and read the Bible. Another one refers to the work as *ministry*. And finally, the instructions are for the bishop: "Taking the right hand of each person to be consecrated, and giving the name shall say, *Name*, I admit you to the office of director of Christian education in The Methodist Church, and may God's grace enable you to fulfill the same to his glory."[3] So now we have the terms *office, ministry,* and *consecration* all used in connection with this designation. In addition, when the proceedings of the annual conference refer to the event, it calls it "Commissioning of Director of Christian Education" and then, "Bishop Alton commissioned Miss Corinne Sells as Director of Christian Education" (West Wisconsin Minutes, 1965, 311). So now the term *commission* must be added to the list. All these terms will be relevant to the reordering of ministry in 1996.

In addition, these certified people were relatively free agents in the church. They often moved from one annual conference to another when they were recruited by a different congregation to a new position. For example, Dr. Charles R. Foster was certified as a minister of Christian education in 1964. He recalls graduating from seminary in New York and expecting to return to the Oregon Conference where he grew up. However, he was offered a position in Corning, New York that would focus on educational ministries, and he went there instead. He was ordained as well as certified, but essentially chose where he would be appointed. The bishop agreed, and Foster went to the Methodist Church in Corning. This practice is similar to the system in place for deacons currently; an ordained deacon seeks and finds a place of employment and then requests that the bishop approve it as an appointment.

The staff person on the General Board of Education who administered the certification standards at that time was Rev. R Harold Hipps. As the denomination moved toward merger, Hipps saw a need to form an organization for persons who worked in education ministries. He invited a group of Methodist Christian educators to Estes Park, Colorado in 1966 to form the Christian Educators Fellowship. Sells, who is now the Rev. Corinne Van Buren, had completed a graduate degree in Christian Education, a Master of Arts in Religious Education from Wesley Seminary, and was a certified director of education. Hipps invited her and others like her to come to Estes Park, and she recalls driving across the plains from Wisconsin in a convertible she had just purchased.

Van Buren has powerful memories of that gathering. The workshops were varied, but one she especially enjoyed was on watercolor painting. She also recalls with laughter the day that the participants in the conference took off to travel up the Trail Ridge Road in nearby Rocky Mountain National Park. Because she had this sporty new convertible, several of the staff from the General Board of Education wanted to ride with her. In her flustered state of mind, the ride began with her backing into a post and breaking one of the taillights on her new car. "I had visions of being responsible for killing all of the national staff because I had never driven in the mountains!" she remembers with laughter. The trip did not include any more mishaps, and the conference was a wonderful experience. She recalls that as the conference closed, "*R* [as Hipps was called] had a branding iron in the fire and we all branded a piece of leather with the mark of CEF." The new organization offered a network for training, fellowship, advocacy, and identity formation; CEF became influential and strong for the next several decades, constantly encouraging professional excellence among its members.

One of the goals of the organization was to support laypersons employed by the church who were often without advocates for decent and just employment. After many years in that ministry field myself, I can imagine that some conversations in Estes Park were about senior pastors who were difficult to work with or inadequate salaries. Professional Christian educators, although they were certified and recognized by the conference, had no redress or financial backup from the denomination if they were dismissed or treated unjustly. Many of these persons had graduate level education and years of experience.

Yet, they were at the mercy of church budgets and insecure senior pastors. The CEF organization began to grow. Hipps was an energetic advocate for lay professionals, and he recruited constantly for Christian Educators Fellowship, which was supported by the Board of Education in The Methodist Church and, after 1968, by its successor, the General Board of Discipleship in The United Methodist Church.

The Methodist Church instituted the certification of musicians in 1956 (Division of Diaconal Ministry 1992, 94). After 1960, the title *minister* of music was reserved for ordained persons, but "the 1960 legislation was not retroactive, and persons certified prior to 1960 could retain the title with a notation being made with the listing in the Annual Conference Journal: 'A lay person certified prior to 1960'" (94).[4]

The Fellowship of United Methodists in Music and Worship Arts (FUMMWA) was developing, parallel to CEF, and was supported through the General Board of Discipleship. Like CEF, its members were encouraged to seek professional certification. The organization also advocated for fair employment practices. The president of FUMMWA was a member of the board of directors for the Division of Diaconal Ministry after 1978. FUMMWA worked with the Division on standards for certification.

Another member of Christian Educators Fellowship at its beginning was Rosalie Bentzinger. Then a young Christian educator working in the Iowa conference, Bentzinger remembers that she was tired of hearing Christian educators complain, and R. Hipps encouraged her to run for membership on the national CEF Board. She was elected and eventually became its president: "I learned what was happening for Christian educators [as a member of that board] and I became more and more convinced as I went along that we needed diaconal ministry." As Corinne Van Buren stated, "Having a graduate degree and being treated in such a lowly estate salary-wise did not seem right. I really felt called to do what I was doing, and I wanted the church to include me in its recognized ministry." Dorothy Furnish noted that the understanding of *ministry* was shifting from its association with ordination to the work of all Christians. Furnish observed, "The lay religious educators, who have been seen traditionally as neither lay nor ordained, finally profit from this ambiguous situation, because they can now be understood primarily as persons in ministry" (1976, 110). These issues were at stake at the 1968 merger and in 1996 too, when the General Conference considered a permanent ordained diaconate.

The Consecrated Lay Worker

An initial answer to these concerns was approved in 1968 when the newly formed United Methodist Church included in its organization of ministry the consecrated lay worker, a way to recognize the skilled professionals who were employed by the church, such as Christian educators, administrators, social workers, and musicians. Rena Yocom described it brilliantly when she wrote, "This new consecrated (not ordained) office (not order) of the lay (not ministerial) worker (generalized to fit any profession) was believed sufficient to recognize these emerging church vocations" (1991, 90). Yocom's parenthetical comments point to the issues that remained unresolved. Ordination, clergy status, a ritual of entry, and the range of specialized ministries were at the center of the discussions leading to the General Conference decision of 1996 that established the ordained deacon. The consecrated lay worker was a significant step on the journey but far from a true recognition of specialized ministries!

Should these people—who are clearly doing ministry but not entitled to be called *minister*, who are employed by the church but only on an individual contract basis, who have no identifiable place in the annual conference or relationship to the bishop, who have graduate-level education and are accomplished in their ministerial skills, who have met the standards for professional certification set by the denomination, who belong to no order or group for accountability, and who are answering a call to ministry—be accorded support systems such as pension and a defined place in the annual conference? F. Thomas Trotter, General Secretary of the General Board of Higher Education and Ministry observed, "By 1968 . . . it had become apparent that the lay worker was a specialized minister but without some of the support systems accorded by the church to the ordained ministry" (Keller 1987, viii). The new office was conferred upon a candidate through *consecration,* just as the professional certification was. To consecrate usually means to set apart or dedicate for a sacred purpose. Buildings were consecrated. Bishops were consecrated. Directors and ministers of Christian education or music were consecrated. Now lay workers would be consecrated. Clearly, the lay worker of 1968 did not arise from nothing. It was an expansion of the professional certifications and offered a broader range of options for recognized lay ministries than were currently available for certification. And it was recognized by consecration, which set the lay worker apart for ministry.

One of those most responsible for the creation of the consecrated lay worker was the Rev. R. Harold Hipps, who had been the champion of Christian educators. The structure of the new denomination placed the lay worker under the new General Board of Higher Education and Ministry (GBHEM), and Hipps moved from the former Board of Education to become the head of the GBHEM Division of Lay Ministry.

The 1968 *Discipline* defines the lay worker in ¶501: "a person other than the clergy whose decision to make a career of work (either full-time or term) in the employed status in the Church or church-related agencies is accompanied by the meeting of standards of excellence in the chosen field of service and who has been consecrated by a bishop." Paragraph 502 states that a lay worker must be a member in good standing of a congregation and present evidence of good health. In some conferences, psychological testing was required for the candidate. In addition, a candidate needed to be certified by the annual conference. The consecration service could be combined with the service of ordination at annual conference.

That paragraph foreshadows the eventual decision in 1996 to ordain persons who work at the specialized ministries this consecrated lay worker office encompassed. However, the lay worker was carefully designated as a layperson, not ordained. Even the choice of the title "worker" indicated a choice not to use the term "minister," which at that time was reserved for members of an annual conference who were ordained (Yocom 1991, 88).

Ecumenical Advocacy for a Renewed Diaconate and Vatican II Actions

Christianity, which had fractured and fractured again since its beginnings in the first century, began to dream of coming together again after the end of World War II. Exciting and optimistic visions of Christianity unifying around the globe were emerging in ecumenical dialogues. Part of the work that might lead to this new unity involved defining basic doctrine and understandings of ministry. These discussions included consideration of the role of *diakonia* in ministry, particularly in response to the needs of the world.

The World Council of Churches resumed its work in 1948 following World War II (The United Nations was formed in 1945) and included many Protestant and Eastern Orthodox Christian denominations. The National Council of Churches of Christ in the USA (NCC) was formed in 1950 with the intention of being a "leading voice of witness to the living Christ" (https://national councilofchurches.us/about-us/) through education and advocacy. The Consultation on Church Union began in 1962 with hope for more mergers in the United States. One evidence of this hope was The United Methodist Church, formed in 1968 by joining two American Protestant denominations with Wesleyan roots.

Methodists participated eagerly in the ecumenical movement. The Reverend Gerald Moede, a Methodist elder, was part of these ecumenical dialogues about similarities and differences. Moede was on the Commission on Faith and Order of the World Council of Churches for seven years. Later he would serve as General Secretary of the Consultation on Church Union, an ecumenical group in the United States. Many of these ecumenical discussions centered on how the various communions understood their sacramental theology and how they ordered ministry. The World Council of Churches realized that the unity they were striving for would need to come to some agreement on the theology and practices of baptism, eucharist, and ministry. The result of their ecumenical dialogue was *Baptism, Eucharist, and Ministry*, published in 1982. This document remains important; the 2020 report of the Commission to Study Ministry quotes it.

The World Council of Churches' conversations about ministry revealed some significant differences but also coalesced around three set-apart forms: bishop, presbyter, and the diaconate or deacon. Many of the participants in the ecumenical dialogue had some form of ordained priest or presbyter; some had bishops, but some did not; the diaconate, the form of ministry in which the deacon resides, took many forms, but most deacons and deaconesses were not ordained. Therefore, the deacon and its role in church leadership received considerable attention. Research had revealed that the early church deacons had a variety of roles and authority, which waxed and waned over the first few centuries. The work of James Monroe Barnett is particularly helpful and comprehensive in its survey of this history. In *The Diaconate: A Full and Equal Order*, first published in 1981, he investigates the various historical versions of *diakonia*. While he finds that *diakonia* was understood as the ministry of all people who followed Jesus, Christian groups began to identify an office of deacon with various roles in different centuries. At times it was subservient to the presbyter, with deacons serving as apprentice priests. At other times, using Barnett's phrase, it was a "full and equal order" along with the presbyter (217). The proposal from the World Council of Churches and its Faith and Order group was for the diaconate as a full and equal order alongside the bishop and presbyter/elder.

The Roman Catholic Church led the way in restoring a permanent diaconate in the twentieth century. Pope John XXIII began the movement by convening the Second Vatican Council in 1961, urging it to consider how to bring the church into the modern world. Perhaps the most famous outcomes of that council were the decree that the mass should be spoken in the language of the culture and the expanded leadership of the laity. In addition, the council restored a permanent diaconate under the direction and supervision of its bishops (Keller 1987, 54–55). Pope Paul VI declared, in a 1967 apostolic letter, that the diaconate "is not to be considered as a mere step toward the priesthood, but it is so adorned with its own indelible character and its own special grace so that those who are called to it can permanently serve the mysteries of Christ and the Church."

Christian bodies that sought opportunities for cooperation and unity were watching and listening as all this ecumenical work proceeded. A permanent diaconate was under consideration in most of the mainline Protestant denominations, and that influence was quite strong in The United Methodist Church.

Methodist Efforts to Define Ordination, Ministry, and the Mission of the Church

Discussions about reclaiming the diaconate as a part of ordained ministry in Christian churches were undergirded by a renewed understanding of the church as the "people of God." By our baptism, we are all called to ministry or *diakonia*. *Baptism, Eucharist, and Ministry* begins the section on ministry with a heading: "The Calling of the Whole People of God." These baptized ones are then "to identify with the joys and sufferings of all people as they seek to witness in caring love. The members of Christ's body are to struggle with the oppressed towards that freedom and dignity promised with the coming of the Kingdom" (World Council of Churches [WCC] 1982, 20). The presbyters, deacons, and bishops provide leadership for the people of God.

The Methodist Church was not immune to the ideas generating in the ecumenical discussions and continued to ask for study of those ideas. Richard P. Heitzenrater, a Wesleyan historian, was asked to write a history of its ministry studies. He found one as early as 1944, but he described the early studies as "sociological and demographic studies" (1988, 1). He also noted that the 1964 report asserted "that the term minister should be reserved for those who are ordained and in full connection" (3). The General Conference did not approve the 1964 report but instead authorized a new study. That study, offered to the General Conference of the new denomination in 1968, emphasized the interconnectedness of ordination and sacrament. It retained the sequential ordination of deacon prior to elder. This meant that the practice of the former Methodist Church prevailed over the practice of the Evangelical United Brethren.

More significant than that may be a shift in that report to a new use of the term *minister*. Paragraph 301 begins: "Ministry in the Christian church is derived from the ministry of Christ. . . . All Christians are called to ministry, and theirs is a ministry of the people of God within the community of faith and in the world," The next paragraph states, "There are persons within the ministry of the baptized who are called of God and set apart by the Church for the specialized ministry of Word, Sacrament, and Order." This theological understanding of ministry as the calling of the whole people of God becomes the beginning point for answering this question from *Baptism, Eucharist, and Ministry*: "How, according to the will of God and under the guidance of the Holy Spirit, is the life of the Church to be understood and ordered, so that the Gospel may be spread and the community built up in love?" (WCC 1982, 20–21).

Part of the answer to this question now, as it was in Acts 6, is to set apart some people with particular gifts and the calling to be leaders. In Acts 6, some disciples are complaining that the food is not being distributed justly to hungry widows. "The Twelve called a meeting of all the disciples and said, 'It isn't right for us to set aside proclamation of God's word in order to serve tables. Brothers and sisters, carefully choose seven well-respected men from among you. They must be well-respected and endowed by the Spirit with exceptional wisdom. We will put them in charge of this concern'" (Acts 6:2-3 CEB). The community of those followers of Jesus was organizing itself for certain tasks and identifying leaders, called from the community, to accomplish the work. This passage does not speak of elder, deacon, or ordination; yet it has elements of our practice when persons are authorized and set apart for specific tasks of ministry; they receive prayer and the laying on of hands.

In the twenty centuries since the events in Acts, the church has organized its leadership in a variety of ways. At times, ministry was the responsibility of the entire community. At other times, the priest took over and the people looked on. When The United Methodist Church was constituted, ministry had become the work of the whole people of God. The EUB practice of a single ordination for elders was overruled. In the Methodist Church, men and women seeking to become elders were ordained first as deacons and a second time when they became elders with full membership in the annual conference. The deaconess office was still an option for laywomen. And local pastors who completed the Course of Study and had served under appointment for some time, could become deacons, but they were associate members of the annual conference and could not vote on all matters. These were essentially permanent deacons, although that terminology does not appear in the *Discipline.* People with skills and training in specialized ministries could be certified and then consecrated as a lay worker.

The Book of Discipline (1968) defines three classifications of persons who "exercise certain pastoral functions." The first paragraph describes elders as "ministers" who have been elected to full membership in the annual conference and ordained after completing their formal education (¶307.1). It continues, "Deacons are ministers who have progressed sufficiently in their preparation for the ministry to be received by an Annual Conference as either probationary members or associate members" (¶307.2). Paragraph 307.3 describes lay pastors who must be licensed and approved each year by the Annual Conference. Reading through these paragraphs one finds that the term *minister* is still being used to indicate the persons who serve the church as pastors; the new notion that all Christians are called to be ministers has not quite taken hold.

These paragraphs were part of chapter 2, "The Ministry," in the *Discipline.* Chapter 3, which described the new lay-worker category, declined to use the term *minister* and instead consistently used *worker.* The opening description relies on a negative to distinguish this person, who probably appeared to most observers to be doing ministry. "A lay worker in the Church is a person, other than the clergy, whose decision to make a career of work (either full-time or term) in the employed status" (¶501). As Rena Yocom pointed out, the effort to avoid using minister in the description seems labored. The description then says that the lay worker *"has been consecrated by a bishop"* (emphasis mine). It still sounds a lot like ministry. Why would the bishop consecrate someone for work that is not ministry! The lay worker was to be seated with voice but not vote in the annual conference, and was also to be in relationship with a charge conference. These decisions regarding the lay-worker category danced up closely to the descriptions of the elder and deacon but then stepped back, just a little. The church was beginning to discern the need to set apart some persons with skills for specialized areas of ministry so that, as *Baptism, Eucharist, and Ministry* said, "the Gospel may be spread, and the community built up in love" (WCC 1982, 20–21).

The 1968 General Conference followed the lead of six preceding conferences and authorized a Commission for the Study of Ministry that was to report to the 1972 General Conference. Heitzenrater (1988, 5) reports that the commission spent much of its time considering how to distribute theological education; how many seminaries were needed and where they should be located. In addition, it designed the administrative structure of the new denomination, creating a General Board of Higher Education and Ministry that would relate to colleges, universities, and seminaries, and to ministry. The board was to have four divisions: Ordained Ministry, Lay Ministry, Higher Education, and Chaplains and Related Ministry. Thus, the consecrated lay worker was moved into this board, and R. Harold Hipps was moved from the Board of Education to lead it in 1972.

In 1968, the new denomination was born with a grand vision for unity. Its optimism stood in contrast to the turmoil present in the culture of the United States. As more and more voices in the culture demanded equal rights for women, an end to racial segregation, and an end to the war in Vietnam, voices in the church also shifted the notion of ministry from the work of ordained clergy to the work of all the people of God. Traditional theologies were expanded by liberation theologies. The church began, too slowly, to divest itself of its racial divisions and to make space for women among the ordained leadership. The consecrated lay worker offered a more defined place in the denomination for those whose call was not to the priestly work of elder. The name of this office also made space for a broader definition of the kinds of leaders who were needed. Lay workers were most often located in the fields of Christian education, evangelism, social work, and music, but this more generic term also allowed for other specializations. The ecumenical renewal of the diaconate was well underway in Roman Catholic, Protestant, and Orthodox churches. Whether most United Methodists were conscious of it or not, this movement was seeping from ecumenical dialogues and percolating into the vision of how The United Methodist Church could order its leadership. The lay worker—certified, consecrated, and commissioned—was an important early step toward the vision that would be enacted in 1996.

2 Creating the Consecrated Diaconal Minister

With the action of the 1972 General Conference, the new denomination entered another new phase. The General Agencies were formed, and their staff were put in place. The new logo with a cross and flame was installed on many church buildings and at the top of church stationeries. People were learning to say that they were *United* Methodists, even though they sometimes forgot. The UMC was poised for intensified ministry. Optimism was abundant.

Finally, the dissolution of the segregated Central Jurisdiction of The Methodist Church was completed, and its congregations were merged with conferences that overlapped geographically. The United Methodist Church, sadly, did not lead the way in this work of addressing its systemic racism. The American public schools had been challenged to address racial segregation since the landmark Supreme Court decision in Brown vs. Board of Education in 1954. The Civil Rights Act was signed into law by President Lyndon B. Johnson in 1968. Still, the White majority was dragging its feet and resisting on multiple fronts. As the Civil Rights movement began to prompt changes in the public sphere, pressure was building for the church to eliminate its segregated Central Jurisdictional Conference. Therefore, in 1968, the two denominations affirmed their intention to unite as equals, including the African American congregations of the Central Jurisdiction, The Evangelical United Brethren, and the Methodist Church. The United Methodist Church was launched.

Despite the cultural excitement about grassroots power and the value of listening to voices from the margins, the new denomination was organized like a smaller version of the United States' government. It would be a representative democracy with majority rule. A denominational structure was approved with the General Conference as the only body that could speak for the church, and it was dominated by White American males. The General Conference writes and revises *The Book of Discipline*, which contains theological and organizational rules. General Conference meets every four years and is the church's primary legislative body. General Conference has the authority to make rules and speak for the whole church. The structure also includes a Judicial Council, similar to the Supreme Court. The executive branch is divided between a Council of Bishops and various general agencies, commissions, and councils. Four administrative program agencies were established to help the church accomplish its mission: The General Board of Global Ministries, The General Board of Discipleship, The General Board of Church and Society, and The General Board of Higher Education and Ministry. With the new organization defined, all was prepared for the approved agencies to organize and hire staff.

At the local church level, the new denomination simply retained many offices for lay leadership from the structures and offices of both the former Methodist and Evangelical United Brethren churches. Ambiguity and duplication were everywhere in this plan. For example, the office of Sunday school superintendent (from the Methodists) and the age-level coordinators for children, youth, and adults (from the Evangelical United Brethren) were still listed in the *Discipline* in the section on the local church. As a fledgling Christian educator, I was hired in 1978 to run the program ministries of a large congregation and asked to recruit people for all these overlapping offices. Trying to describe how they related to one another was challenging. Despite so much remaining unresolved, the new denomination was hopeful as it began to settle into the new structures—hopeful it could make a difference in the lives of people and of the nation and globe.

The General Board of Higher Education and Ministry and the Commission for the Study of Ministry, 1972–1976

Two of the new structures established in 1972 are particularly relevant to the development of the ministry legislation in 1996: The General Board of

Higher Education and Ministry and the Commission for the Study of Ministry 1972–1976.

The consecrated lay worker that was initiated in 1968 was attracting some gifted and skilled professionals who were employed by the church and its agencies. In what was to prove important for the church's permanent diaconate and 1996 action, a young woman named Rena Yocom was interested in the office. Yocom had graduated from Central Methodist College in Fayette, Missouri in 1965, and was employed by a church in Kansas City to lead its Christian Education program. R. Harold Hipps, staff at the General Board of Education, encouraged her to take more courses so she could meet the standards to be certified as associate in Christian education. She traveled to several Methodist graduate schools to complete the requirements and was certified in 1970. In 1971, she was consecrated as a lay worker by the Kansas East Conference. Thus, Yocom was taking courses, applying, and being affirmed for these specialized, nonordained, denominational categories during the first quadrennium of the new United Methodist denomination.

In 1972, the new General Board of Higher Education and Ministry was approved by the General Conference. Rena Yocom's story of how she became one of the elected directors of this general board is one that still seems to take her a bit by surprise. She had been nominated by the Kansas East Conference to the pool of persons eligible to serve on the general agencies. The pool identified each nominee by a category: layperson, clergyman, and clergywoman. The membership of a board of directors had to be balanced with representatives from each category, with attention to racial and ethnic diversity, as well as from each jurisdiction. (A version of this quota process is still in place in 2021.) Yocom did not expect to be tapped because the Kansas East Conference delegation had placed a clergyman from her conference at the top of their list. As it turned out, he was elected as a bishop by the jurisdictional conference later that summer. Thus, he was no longer eligible. When a laywoman was needed for balance on the board, Rena Yocom's name rose to the top of the list, and she became a director on the new General Board of Higher Education and Ministry when the agency was organized in the fall of 1972.

When the new directors of the General Board of Higher Education and Ministry (GBHEM) convened, they were separated into four divisions that related to the same divisions in the board staffing: Ordained Ministry, Lay Ministry, Higher Education, and Chaplains and Related Ministries. Dr. Ethel Johnson, a professor of Christian education, was also elected to that board.

She recalls, "I chaired the Division of Lay Ministers. This was a new division. It lasted only one quadrennium. I remember nobody else wanted to be on the division of lay ministers because they thought it was nothing" (Johnson, 2012). Yocom was also assigned to the Division of Lay Ministry. This was a natural fit since she had recently been consecrated as a lay worker, which would be a responsibility of that division. R Hipps knew Yocom because she was one of the people who had met the qualifications to be consecrated in the new office of lay worker only two years before. I imagine that he may have suggested to the directors that they should include this bright and articulate young woman from the middle of the country in their executive leadership. Hipps never seems to have missed an opportunity to advocate for the people he had come to know and appreciate who served in the field of Christian education. Yocom was subsequently elected as secretary of the Division of Lay Ministry.

The inclusion of a young woman, newly consecrated to the office of lay worker, on the very first denominational body responsible for administering the standards and processes for ordained and consecrated lay ministries proved providential. Yocom's presence was to have a big impact on both the discussions leading to the 1976 General Conference and the eventual decision in 1996 to create a new form of deacon. United Methodists like me are inclined to see this sort of thing as the work of the Holy Spirit. Yocom was beginning to discern a call to a form of ministry that did not yet exist formally, and she helped others envision its promise.

The 1972 General Conference also authorized another Study of Ministry Commission with instructions to report back to General Conference in 1976. It became known as the "Cannon Commission" after Bishop William Ragsdale Cannon who chaired it. The commission was formally constituted at the 1972 fall meeting of the Council of Bishops. When the commission agreed to consider a permanent diaconate the next spring, two people were added to the commission as consultants. One was Rena Yocom, representing the Division of Lay Ministry from GBHEM. The other was Betsy Ewing, staff person for Deaconesses and Home Missionaries at the General Board of Global Ministries. Deaconesses were, of course, laywomen; they had a century of ministry history in addressing education, poverty, and health.

Heitzenrater described this commission's work as "a radical shift in the church's view of ministry" (1988, 5). Thomas E. Frank, then a young student at Candler School of Theology at Emory University, also served on that commission. Frank writes, "Those were heady days in reformation of the ordained ministry, partly in relation to COCU [Consultation on Church Union] on discussions in which I was a 'young adult' delegate." The new denomination was anxious to find ways to join the ecumenical consensus as it made decisions about its structure and leadership.

In the 1972 *Discipline*, a sentence in the middle of ¶310 on the nature of ministry stated, "All Christians are called to ministry." However, the term *ministry* had been declared some years before as applicable only to the work of those who are ordained. "Some strong lay voices on the commission argued *they* were real *ministers*, not the clergy," Yocom remembers. The laity argued that their daily lives were settings for ministry. The commission was applying the four theological sources and guidelines of Scripture, tradition, experience, and reason, known informally as the Wesleyan quadrilateral. After considerable discussion, they found that a theological argument could not be made that limited the term *ministry* to the work of ordained persons. They began to use adjectives to distinguish between the *general ministry* of all the baptized and the *representative ministry* of the ordained. The notion that *minister* should be applied only to clergy and everybody else was *laity* "really got bounced in that commission," remembers Yocom.

Yocom recalls "a lot of talking about grassroots power. It was a time that we began talking about women's rights. All of those ideas entered into the conversation of the ministry commission." This reflected the movement in Western culture away from top-down hierarchies and toward grassroots empowerment. Another commission member, Max Marble, who was a seminary student at the time, remembers "advocating for a change in terminology in the *Discipline* about ministers. It had long troubled me how the *Discipline* referred to ministers and laypersons as if laypersons in the church did not have a calling to ministry. My district superintendent considered me quite the thorn in his flesh by my insisting that laypersons were ministers."

Members of the commission were young and influenced by the cultural conversations of the day. Their progressive approach seems like another evidence of the Holy Spirit inspiring change in the church. Thomas E. Frank, who subsequently became one of the foremost scholars of the denomination's polity and mission, says that "putting ministry of all Christians first before other chapters [of the *Discipline*] was the breakthrough in structure—and theology—of the book, a profound reshaping of the context of ordination, and we were very excited about that."

With some clarity about *ministry*, the discussion also considered a permanent diaconate. This too was in line with its desire to find points of consensus with the ecumenical dialogues that were hoping to revive the *deacon* as a form of ministry. The General Board of Higher Education and Ministry directors hired a new general secretary, The Rev. Dr. F. Thomas Trotter. He supported the commission's consideration of a permanent diaconate for United Methodism. So did Dr. Robert W. Thornburg, associate general secretary of the Division of the Ordained Ministry, who had just joined the staff. Rena Yocom's memories of these discussions remain vivid, even after nearly fifty years:

> The question came down to what to do about the permanent diaconate. We had two forms of deacon already at that point. One form of deacon, which was what we later called the transitional deacon, was the steppingstone to elder. There was also the ordained deacon who was an associate member of the annual conference; that deacon was a lay pastor. We began to call them local pastors, because their authority was local. They became associate members and were ordained deacon.

The commission could not come to an agreement in using the term *deacon*. Frank recalls heated discussions. "I don't remember who proposed the term *diaconal ministry*, but it was definitely a compromise given that most commission members did not want to give up the order of deacon as a step toward elder." The two-step ordination of transitional deacon and then elder was all that ordained clergy in the Methodist branch of the UMC had known. Yocom also remembers passionate discussion:

> The first vote was on whether we could have multiple kinds of deacons. Could we have transitional deacons, permanent deacons, and whatever the associate member would be called? By a vote of 13 to 12 they voted that the denomination could not handle that kind of confusion. [So, a permanent *deacon* was not on the table.]
>
> Betsy [Ewing] and I were a part of the whole discussion, and they made time for each of us to address how we understood our ministry either as deaconess or consecrated lay worker. In my presentation I used H. Richard Niebuhr's four calls, not only the secret call.[1] Then you really begin to live out that call in a particular way, but you are waiting for the ecclesial affirmation of that call. I think some were intrigued by that.

Then they appointed a smaller group to think through other possibilities. They put me in that group. Also, in that group were Bishop Holter and Bishop Stowe who both knew me. I was probably in my late twenties by then. I was kind of brash. I really didn't realize the impact [of these considerations]. I really didn't. I was just doing what I had been asked to do. Anyway, I think Don Holter was looking at me and said he would like to hear from Rena. And I kind of shook my head. I was a little bit intimidated. And Bishop Stowe said, "Go ahead, Rena." And finally, I said, "Does this mean in Niebuhr's terms there is no authentication or verification of the form of ministry that I do? There is no place in the church to recognize the ministry of folks like us?" And there was just stone quiet. And Bishop Stowe, who had this kind of Texas drawl, said, "What we need is an adjectival form of the word *deacon*." And Bishop Roy Short, who was a bishop in Florida at that time, said, "Well that would be *DEEaconal* or *DAIaconal* depending on where you learned Greek." And we all laughed at that, but we kept coming back to it because we couldn't find another solution. And then they started jokes about "if its diagonal."

The committee brought this back to the larger ministry committee. . . . If it is an adjective, you would have the general ministry, the ordained ministry, the consecrated ministry, and the diaconal ministry. We floated that it would be a consecrated ministry because we had the consecrated lay worker and deaconesses were consecrated, but the bishops wouldn't stand to have two consecrated ministries. Because we couldn't find a better solution, we took it to the whole committee, and it passed. Not by much but it passed. It kept it as a lay office which made the deaconess happy. That commission really did a phenomenal job to pull this together in a coherent form when the denomination was very new.

The work of the Cannon Commission was approved by the 1976 General Conference with relative ease. Yocom recalls that the Council of Bishops and the General Board of Higher Education and Ministry supported its proposals. "There wasn't any big group to challenge it," recalls Yocom. "Even the paragraph that said, 'no ministry is subservient to another.' Boy, we fought for that!" she remembers. Thus, diaconal ministry, the next step toward the ordained deacon, was born.

The Division of Lay Ministry at GBHEM was renamed the Division of Diaconal Ministry, and paragraphs 301–399 in the 1976 *Discipline* were devoted to the new Diaconal Ministry. Yocom also remarked that human sexuality was an item of discussion for first time at the 1976 General Conference, and perhaps so much energy went to that debate that the diaconal ministry proposal received little attention.

As we look back on the groundbreaking work of this commission, it becomes obvious that a lot of things had to come together to end up with the proposal of the diaconal minister. The commission had several young leaders appointed to it who were committed to the grassroots power notions of the times. And two of the bishops knew young Rena Yocom and made space for her voice to be heard. Tom Frank later emerged as a foremost scholar of United Methodist polity and mission. He knew the church from the inside as the son of a bishop. His voice was part of the mix. Max Marble was the son of a Methodist missionary who grew up in India and had deep commitments to the marginalized and poor. Their stories embody the perspectives of many others who contributed to this decision. The values of the late 1960s, with all the turmoil over war and racial injustice and the increasing movement to give power and voice to the grassroots, were in the room during all the discussions.

Diaconal Ministry Is Born

The action of the 1976 General Conference in Portland, Oregon created a new section in the *Book of Discipline*, "The Diaconal Ministry." Chapter 3 is short, but it stands alone, parallel to the much longer chapter 4 on ordained ministry. The first paragraph explains that the various current forms of diaconal ministry—deaconess, home missionary, and lay worker—are "recognized as having been called to the diaconal ministry" (¶301). Apparently, the intent was to combine several earlier designations of *diakonia* into the new office.

In 1976, Jimmy Carter defeated Gerald Ford, who had become president in the wake of the Watergate scandal and Nixon's resignation. Americans were suspicious of people in power. Corruption was in the cultural background as the General Conference approved its new statement on the ministry of all Christians. Thomas Trotter, in his annual report to GBHEM (the *Yearbook*), called it "an eloquent product of the board's effort to deepen and broaden the theological definitions of ministry" (GBHEM 1976, 20). Diaconal ministry was integrally connected to this idea.

Paragraph 301 (*Discipline* 1976) continues, "Within the total Church community there are persons called of God and set apart through consecration for specialized ministries of service in the Church's life and mission. These are consecrated diaconal ministers." Some bishops had resisted having another form of ministry that would be consecrated, but that did not prevail; the new diaconal minister would be consecrated. As so often happens in the *Discipline*, the assertion that diaconal ministers have a divine call and are set apart seems to be contradicted by the language in ¶303, "whose decision to make a professional career in the employed status in The United Methodist Church or its related agencies." The calling and covenantal aspect named in the earlier paragraph disappears into professionalism. General Secretary of GBHEM, Tom Trotter, commented to the directors in 1976 that "Diaconal Ministry is the great new concept for professional ministry. The inexorable pressure from the lay professional for status, equity, and professional recognition in The United Methodist Church created the conditions" and a new office was born (GBHEM 1976, 19). In contrast, Rosalie Bentzinger, who would soon head up the Division of Diaconal Ministry, commented that "Diaconal Ministers have not created themselves; they are a product of the church's desire to be in mission" (1991, 4). Both the pressure for recognition of professionals who served the church and the church's desire to recognize the role of laity in its mission contributed to the impetus for this new office.

Three categories of characteristics—personal, ecclesial, and professional/educational—qualified one to be a diaconal minister. The personal category included Christian faith, church membership, physical and mental health, character, and "willingness and ability to work with persons of various social, religious, and ethnic backgrounds" (*Discipline* 1976, ¶305.2.a). This final requirement reflects the turmoil of the times and the church's commitment to diversity as it became less segregated. Surprisingly, *race* is not included in the sentence. The ecclesial standards required each candidate to be a member in good standing of the UMC along with knowing and supporting the doctrine and polity of the denomination (*Discipline* 1976, ¶305.2.b). Professionally, the candidate for consecration as a diaconal minister needed to have been certified, which required advanced education, and employed full time in a church or church agency for at least a year (*Discipline* 1976, ¶305.3). These qualifications were not much different from those required of candidates for lay worker, but the "diaconal ministry" term seemed to elevate it along with the language of being called and set apart.

The diaconal minister's role in the annual conference also expanded a bit from that of the lay worker. The diaconal minister was eligible to serve as a layperson on committees of the annual conference and to be elected as a lay delegate to General or Jurisdictional Conferences. Also, the diaconal minister could be a voting member of the annual conference when elected by the congregation in which their membership resided or as part of the lay equalization plan.

Another small step toward recognition of the call and vocation of diaconal ministers came with ¶308, which gave the resident bishop where the diaconal minister was employed the responsibility to appoint him or her. The diaconal minister had to find a place of employment and be recommended by the Board of Diaconal Ministry, but ultimately the bishop would make the appointment. Putting the authority for appointment in the hands of the bishop made diaconal ministers somewhat parallel to elders and local pastors who also received an appointment from the bishop.

The action of 1976 created an office named "diaconal minister," described it as called and set apart, gave it professional status, defined its role in a charge conference and the annual conference, and asked the bishop to appoint the minister. The ritual for consecration was to be part of a worship service. The diaconal ministers were asked to answer questions of faith and covenant. Then, while the candidate was kneeling at the altar rail, a bishop would lay on hands and say the words of consecration. The lay workers had usually been consecrated during the annual conference session (as Corinne Van Buren was in 1974), so moving it into a worship setting elevated it. With this ritual of consecration, the diaconal minister looked a lot like the other clergy of the conference to an untrained eye. However, diaconal ministry remained a lay office through consecration rather than ordination. Diaconal ministers chose the basin and towel as their symbol. Most also chose to wear an alb, a traditional garment that does not signify any heightened status. Over the alb, they wore the traditional deacon's stole, which hangs from the left shoulder to the right hip.

Looking back, Tom Frank says, "I do recall thinking that 'diaconal ministry' was a made-up name and category that was just going to float outside of any office or membership or ritual, and of course, that proved to be the case. I thought the UMC should either do deacon or not do deacon, make a clean decision, and move on." This may not have been a clean decision, but it was clearly a step toward an ordained diaconate.

The General Board of Higher Education and Ministry, Division of Diaconal Ministry

In 1972, one of the first tasks of the General Board of Higher Education and Ministry directors had been to hire a general secretary. They chose Dr. F. Thomas Trotter who had deep experience in theological education and in the church. In the 1974 *Yearbook*, Trotter's report to the board was direct about the challenges: "I would be less than honest with you if I suggested that this year we bring to a close was unruffled and without dissonance . . . This time last year we were several agencies, cut adrift by General Conference decisions many of us did not understand, and put together like some giant Dagwood sandwich into this new Board of Higher Education and Ministry" (16–17). Joaquin Garcia, who later joined GBHEM staff, recalled that Trotter "was able to give us the big picture, almost in a poetic way, with a sense of humor, vision, and hope." By 1976 Trotter's report was hopeful about diaconal ministry, and he was assembling a staff to support it.

When Trotter was appointed as general secretary, the Division of Lay Ministry was still led by associate general secretary R. Harold Hipps. Edith Goodman was working with him as director of conference relations. However, the General Conference of 1976 approved the office of diaconal minister with the intention that it would supplant the consecrated lay worker. Trotter had supported this creation of a permanent diaconate for the church, and he saw the need to hire staff who embodied the new office.

Trotter recruited Rosalie Bentzinger as GBHEM staff for the new Division of Diaconal Ministry. She had been serving on the staff of the Iowa conference as a Christian educator. She had joined the conference staff after completing a master's degree in the Christian education program of Garrett-Evangelical Theological Seminary and Northwestern University. She was content there but recalls that Trotter "just kept calling" her. He knew her because she had been elected to the board of Christian Educators Fellowship for which Hipps continued to provide support through his position in the Division of Lay Ministry. Then she was elected CEF president. After the 1976 General Conference, Bentzinger had been encouraged to become a diaconal minister. R. Harold Hipps was the first associate general secretary for the Division of Diaconal Ministry, but he was an ordained elder. Bentzinger remembers that Trotter wanted a diaconal minister in that office. Trotter wanted her "to work toward a stronger diaconate in the UMC." But he also "tried to be fair," she remembers. In 1979, Rosalie Bentzinger joined the staff as associate general secretary for the Division of Diaconal Ministry, renamed from Lay Ministry.

In 1979, Joaquin Garcia, also a newly consecrated diaconal minister and Christian educator, was recruited to join the staff as director of Conference Relations. He shared that his responsibilities were:

1. Work with the Conferences to form and train the Conference Boards of Diaconal Ministry. In 1979 there were 73 Annual Conferences.[2] In 1979, only one third of the conferences had organized Conference Boards of Diaconal Ministry. Joaquin worked to develop the *Handbook for Conference Boards of Diaconal Ministry.*

2. Prepare for the 1980 General Conference and keep track of petitions and legislation related to diaconal ministry; try to identify delegates to General Conference who were supportive of diaconal ministry and open to the concept of the Order of Deacon in order to expand the network.

3. Develop brochures describing the personal, theological, educational, and Church requirements for diaconal ministry, and other similar resources.

4. Plan for the five jurisdictional training events for conference Boards of Diaconal Ministry.

5. As the director of Conference Relations, train conference Boards of Diaconal Ministry.

The five responsibilities listed make it clear that the staff of GBHEM was taking a position that supported diaconal ministry and hoped to convince the UMC to create an ordained deacon order. Garcia recalls that they

> . . . encouraged every Conference Board of Diaconal Ministry to send at least 3 persons to the jurisdictional training events to help build a cadre of mutual support in their conference to interpret Diaconal Ministry and professional certification. The concept was for the local churches and annual conferences to recognize God's call to persons to ministries of service and justice, and to equip the church to serve the community and the world. Doing this led into greater awareness of the uniqueness of call and response, and how equipping, fulfilling the personal, theological, educational, and church requirements, and areas of specialized ministry could be developed. The Conference Boards were very innovative as to how to interpret diaconal ministry using different means and

media to reach out to Bishops, laity, clergy, district superintendents and council directors.

The Division of Diaconal Ministry was advocating for diaconal ministry and helping conferences organize their new boards, but its underlying goal was to move to an order of ordained deacon in the UMC. As associate general secretary of the division, Bentzinger soon realized that her Division of Diaconal Ministry and the Division of Ordained Ministry were "diametrically opposed." Staff in the Division of Ordained Ministry were resisting the work of her division. "Some thought we were going to destroy the ordained elder or ordained ministry." Some thought "these people are interlopers of some kind." The Division of Chaplains was on the fence and did not clearly join either camp, Eventually, Bentzinger realized that "I could not get hysterical about it. It was just going to take time."

Garcia remembers this tension too. "The General Secretary of the GBHEM, Thomas Trotter, always reminded us that we should not be concerned about *territoriality*! Instead, we and the whole church needed to remember that 'there is enough need in the world to go around!'"

Bentzinger recalls, "Each General Conference brought us a little closer to our goal."

The Committee to Study Diaconal Ministry, 1976–1980

The division came into focus strongly as the Committee to Study Ministry, authorized by the 1976 General Conference, began to meet. According to Rena Yocom, this is how it was constituted:

Bishop Jim Ault, chair of the Division of Ordained Ministry, Claus Rolfe (professor at Perkins and chair of the Division of Chaplains, and I (chair of diaconal ministry) put our heads together and introduced the possibility for GBHEM doing the study—AND requiring all 3 divisions to be at the table. (Chaplains were divided on the issue—some saw their work as "in the world"; however, some (especially women chaplains) saw it as a way to further separate them from the elders in the conference. The "holistic" theme was Jim Ault's special theme song. (Jim had been a prof at Union, NY and then Dean at Drew.) He often quoted 1 Corinthians 12: 7 "To each is given the manifestation of the Spirit for the COMMON good."

The ministry study's task was specifically to flesh out the meaning of diaconal ministry/deacon and how it fit into the total church ministry. Heitzenrater describes this study as a "crucial political maneuver," because the people who would serve on the committee and write the report were all "heavily representative of lay interests in the church" (1988, 6). It "became a turf battle," according to Yocom. Trotter warned that the "unnecessary and even trivializing attention to political and self-serving strategies" must end (GBHEM 1976, 23). He was excited at the possibility for his board staff to do the "conceptual and theological work" (23). Dr. Ethel Johnson co-chaired the study commission along with a person from the General Board of Global Ministries (GBGM). Betsy Ewing, representing the deaconesses, and Rena Yocom were full members of the committee this quadrennium rather than non-voting consultants as they had been in the previous quadrennium. Rosalie Bentzinger and Tom Trotter joined from GBHEM. Gerald F. Moede from COCU brought the ecumenical dimension to their discussion. The general secretaries of two general boards (GBHEM and GBGM) were members along with their staff.

Their report tied both ordained and diaconal ministry to the ministry of Jesus and called them "representative orders." Yocom states that "If we look at the 'whole' of Christ's ministry, the important ministry of bishops and elders at the altar and pulpit cannot be the 'whole' or complete ministry of the church. The diaconate must be seen and recognized." That concept was part of the discussion of the study 1976–1980. The study also broadened the scope of diaconal ministry from its narrower connection to religious education and church music when it wrote, "Diaconal ministry exists to intensify and make more effective the self-understanding of the whole people of God as servants in Christ's name" (DCA 1980, E–27). Diaconal ministers could specialize in a wide variety of ministry and still "intensify and make more effective" (E–27) the ministry of all the people of God.

Just as Trotter was supportive, others were critical of these new ideas. Heitzenrater, for example, was highly critical of what he saw as an inappropriate linkage in this report of "primacy of service (within the general ministry) with the Greek term for service (*diakonia*, sometimes translated as 'servanthood')." Heitzenrater called this linkage a "politicization of scripture to support specific empowerment issues within the structure of the church." He also remarked on "the repetitive 'non-hierarchical' 'non-authoritarian' emphases in this document" (1988, 7).

The growing consensus among United Methodists that all Christians are called to the ministry of Christ shows up strongly in the committee's report! However, the legislative committee that received the report at the 1980 General Conference did not share in these ideas and unanimously recommended nonconcurrence. The report had placed both diaconal ministry and ordained ministry in the category of *representative* ministry, a term that was gaining traction in ecumenical dialogue.

Nevertheless, ¶301 was adopted at the 1980 General Conference. It too pushed the boundary between diaconal ministry and ordained ministry with these words: "The Church also affirms that particular persons are called and set apart for representative ministries of leadership within the body, to help the whole of the membership of the Church be engaged in and fulfill its ministry of service. The purpose of such leadership is the equipping of the general ministry of the Church, to the end that the whole Church may be built up as the body of Christ for the work of ministry." The committee clearly wanted to place diaconal ministry at the center of the ministry of all. This is a far cry from the understanding in 1960 that only ordained persons do ministry. It is also quite different from the language of 1976, which repeatedly referred to diaconal ministers as professionals.

Other 1980 additions to the chapter on diaconal ministry clarified the relationship of diaconal ministers to the annual conference. Like elders, they would be included in leadership of the annual conference.

The qualifications were spelled out more thoroughly, too. The questions that a candidate would be examined on were made parallel to those for candidates for elder seeking full membership in the annual conference but revised to reflect the diaconal ministry. Each of these changes appear to create more parity between diaconal ministry and ordained ministry.

The deaconesses declined to join in the new diaconal ministry, and their office remained with GBGM. They did not want to give up their relationship with bishops and the global diakonia; also, their office had rich historical connections. The office of deaconess is a lay office, now related to United Methodist Women. It has been opened to men too, who are called "home missioners." Deaconesses and home missioners are theologically and professionally trained and devote their lives to full-time service. Deaconesses are another important aspect of the leadership of the church's mission. From the beginning, deaconesses have made a profound difference and contributed to the mission of the transformation of the world.

The legislative committee of the 1980 General Conference voted non-concurrence with the report but also discerned that the ministry divisions of the General Board of Higher Education and Ministry were at odds. Therefore, a new Ministry Study Committee was created. The General Conference appears to have been open to including a permanent diaconate in the representative ministry but was asking for more agreement and coherence from the parties.

When the 1980 General Conference adjourned, the office of diaconal minister was still firmly in place, and its focus was articulated: to lead and equip the ministry of all. The battle between the concepts of ordained and consecrated ministry was not resolved. The advocates for a permanent diaconate were unsatisfied.

3 Continuing to Study and Reflect

The General Conference of 1980 authorized another ministry study for the quadrennium. Although agreeing to support another study is an easy way out of a legislative impasse, the General Conference seems to have understood that more clarification was needed. The 1976 General Conference had renamed the consecrated lay worker as *diaconal minister* and expanded the vision. Four years later, diaconal ministry was gaining acceptance in the wider church, but Joaquin Garcia, who had joined the Division of Diaconal Ministry staff in 1979, said that there was "a sense that diaconal ministry was not yet completed."

The 1980 General Conference instructed the three ministry divisions of GBHEM (diaconal ministry, ordained ministry, and chaplains) to "collaborate" and bring to the General Conference of 1984 recommendations "reflecting a holistic understanding and ordering of ministry with specific response to a permanent diaconate in The United Methodist Church including orders, function, annual conference membership, and itineracy." The new study was instructed to rely on the quadrilateral and be informed by "an ecumenical understanding of ministry for our time" (DCA 1980, 1110). The term *holistic* suggests that the study should provide a comprehensive proposal and that all the ministries of the church needed to be under consideration. In addition, it suggests that the study should focus on designating a set of leaders for the work of *diakonia*. All three ministry divisions of GBHEM were to work together and bring recommendations to the 1984 General Conference.

The terms used in the charge, such as *itineracy* and *conference member-ship*, make it clear that ordination for the diaconal order should be under discussion. The legislative committee that sent the study proposal to the floor wanted this issue to be resolved! In addition, the legislative action stated, "[B]e it further resolved that this interdivisional report is to be completed by October 1, 1982, and then forwarded to the membership and constituencies of the respective divisions for reflection and refinement prior to the 1983 annual meeting of the Board of Higher Education and Ministry where it will be perfected" (DCA 1980, 1110). The repeated discussion of the issue at every General Conference was creating some impatience and desire for resolution.

A Strong GBHEM Staff Promotes Diaconal Ministry

By the 1980s, the understanding that ministry is the work of all baptized Christians was well established, affirming and clarifying that ministry was to take place in their lives in the world. Here and there, across the church, the conviction was growing that a permanent diaconate would help the church to respond more nimbly and effectively to its mission *in the world*. A section in ¶103 of the 1984 *Discipline* titled "The Mission of the Church," states: "God's self-revelation in the life, death, and resurrection of Jesus Christ summons the Church to mission in the world through witness by word and deed." And later in that paragraph it says, "As servants of Christ we are sent into the world to engage in the struggle for justice and reconciliation."

United Methodists were beginning to understand that two forms of ordained clergy might serve the mission better, with one more focused on building up the church where disciples are formed and the other leading the ministries of the church in the world. With this understanding of mission, the argument for an ordained diaconate made sense. In addition, the theological grounding had been established in ¶104: "The heart of Christian ministry is Christ's ministry of outreaching love. Christian ministry is the expression of the mind and mission of Christ." The Gospels provide a clear witness that Jesus' ministry was with people in their ordinary lives. He listened and healed and fed people both literally and spiritually. Jesus's ministry among the people provided the model for a permanent diaconate. As this missional and theological rationale became deeply accepted in United Methodism, the ministry of diakonia appeared to be at the center of what it means to be the church.

At the same time, the Division of Diaconal Ministry, led by Rosalie Bentzinger, was working across the church to get Boards of Diaconal Ministry up and running in every annual conference. Bentzinger was a strong leader. Trotter had found the right person to lead the agency as it helped to develop this new form of ministry for The United Methodist Church. Joaquin Garcia, who worked with her, recalled her commitment to the ministry. "Her integrity and vision were always out front, leading every step of the way! It was not OUR ministry, but that of Jesus Christ." Bentzinger was committed to developing a diverse and inclusive order of deacon for the UMC. Garcia also commented that they did not have computers or cell phones to communicate, and "yet we were able to work in the development of legislation, and able to help bring change."

The Division of Diaconal Ministry invited conference boards to training sessions and provided them with handbooks, all developed by the staff of GBHEM. Joaquin Garcia, who had joined the staff in 1979 as director of Conference Relations, took primary responsibility for this work. In 1979, when Garcia came on board, only one-third of the 73 annual conferences had established a Conference Board of Diaconal Ministry. Some probably did not yet have any diaconal ministers. Garcia and the GBHEM staff were conducting training events in each jurisdiction and encouraging every Conference Board of Diaconal Ministry to send at least three persons. He recalled that "the concept was for the local churches and annual conferences to recognize God's call of persons to ministries of service and justice, and to equip the church to serve the community and the world." They were enlarging and enhancing the vision of the church in the world. Although the educational requirements for diaconal ministers often meant that the candidate chose a relatively narrow field for certification study or a graduate degree, the diaconal ministry was more broadly defined as equipping the people of the church for service.

Those conference boards were also responsible for accepting applications for professional certification and keeping a list of those who were certified. At that time, keeping your certification current required filing an annual report with evidence of continuing education, employment in the field, and recommendation by a supervisor. Certification could be in ministry specialties such as Christian education, evangelism, and church music. Seminaries were invited to Nashville to talk about the courses required for diaconal ministry and certification. They responded by offering the courses in intensive formats as well as in their regular master's degree curricula. Some began to propose more areas for professional certification, and eventually several were approved by GBHEM. Certifications in spiritual formation, youth ministry, and children's ministry were added.[1] Other certifications were envisioned with their focus on the wider community. The seminaries benefited by offering these certification courses, and the church began to gain more and more trained professional leaders for its ministries. With the responsibility for certifications and diaconal ministers, the need for the Conference Board of Diaconal Ministry was evident.

Part of the strategy of the division in Nashville was to keep United Methodists informed about diaconal ministry. Joaquin Garcia and Rosalie Bentzinger realized that it was very important to inform the whole church, not just candidates and boards. Conference boards were encouraged to have a display about diaconal ministry at the annual conference. Those displays could make use of the pamphlets, other printed materials, and media that the division was creating. Press releases about diaconal ministers and what they were doing were solicited. Garcia recalls, "The Conference Boards were very innovative as to how to interpret diaconal ministry using different means and media to reach out to bishops, laity, clergy, district superintendents, and council directors." In addition, Garcia and Bentzinger worked closely with United Methodist Communications and the GBHEM Office of Interpretation. Garcia recalls, "We tried to have a leading article or a news article or a printed resource every three or four months." They succeeded in getting articles into *The Circuit Rider, The Interpreter, Occasional Papers, Newscope, Connections,* and *Colleague*. "Those were very prolific years!"

Seminaries were becoming aware of the diaconal candidates and their need to take graduate-level courses. One way to qualify for diaconal ministry was to complete a theological master's degree such as an MDiv or a Masters in Christian Education. Another route included taking the Basic Graduate Theological Studies courses named in the *Discipline*. In 1984, these consisted of Bible, theology, church history (including United Methodist history), mission of the Church in the world, United Methodist doctrine and polity (*Discipline* 1984, ¶306.3.c). The basic theological courses needed to be combined with either a master's degree in a related field or professional certification. These educational requirements were more flexible than those required for elders, responding to the varied skills and areas of ministry into which God was calling people to diaconal ministry. The Division of Diaconal Ministry was given the responsibility of monitoring and verifying that candidates had met these requirements.

I began taking certification courses in the summer of 1982 at Scarritt Graduate School in Nashville. I had been made aware of the courses at a Christian Educators Fellowship meeting in 1981. I was newly employed by a congregation in Columbia, Missouri as director of Youth and Adult Ministries, temporarily and part time, and was loving the challenge and variety of tasks that were presenting themselves to me. A friend there said, "You should go to Nashville next summer and take a certification course. You would enjoy it!" By the next summer, I was enrolled and spent two weeks taking an intensive course at Scarritt. The community of students and faculty was welcoming and warm. The learning was stimulating, useful for my work, and great fun. I began to learn about both the standards for professional certification and the possibility of diaconal ministry.

I have told the story over and over of how Joaquin Garcia came from his office across the street to the Scarritt campus one afternoon and spoke about the theology of diaconal ministry, the requirements and process of candidacy, and the divine call that we might be experiencing. He believed in the importance of diaconal ministries of love, service, and justice for the work of God's mission in the world. He helped us to see the possibilities too. By my third summer of certification courses, I was seriously considering that I might be called to diaconal ministry. Garcia was doing this sort of teaching and advocacy at most of the United Methodist institutions where certification courses were offered. More people were discerning a call to diaconal ministry. More conferences were establishing a Board of Diaconal Ministry. More diaconal ministers were being consecrated. I was consecrated in 1986 in the Missouri East Conference. In 1986, 1,048 persons were listed as consecrated diaconal ministers in the UMC, and about one thousand more were in candidacy (GBHEM Winter/Spring 1986, 3).

As the numbers began to grow, the competition between the Division of Ordained Ministry and the Division of Diaconal Ministry escalated. General Secretary Tom Trotter saw the possibilities of these new forms of ministry and continued to support the Division of Diaconal Ministry. Bentzinger also believed deeply in the importance of diaconal ministries as critical for the mission of the church. She advocated for funding for the division's work. She stood up to the forces resisting change. Other GBHEM staff were not so sure that diaconal ministry was a good idea.

During these quadrennia, GBHEM began publishing a journal called *Quarterly Review, A Scholarly Journal for Reflection on Ministry*. An article by Jeffrey P. Mickle, then an elder in the Virginia Conference, was published in spring 1982, "Toward a Revised Diaconate." He begins with the conviction that "Any consideration of the church's orders of ministry should be made only in relation to its function as extender of the ministry of its Lord" (Mickle, 44). This echoes Bentzinger's stance that diaconal ministry is a ministry of Jesus Christ.

The 1980–1984 Ministry Study

The instruction to the staff of the ministry divisions of GBHEM that they consult with their "members and constituencies" presented a particular challenge for the Division of Diaconal Ministry. The number of persons who had been consecrated as diaconal ministers by that time was very small compared to the number of ordained elders and the probationary deacons who were on their way to elder's orders. Most laity had never met a diaconal minister, had little knowledge of what they did, and were not sure that such a thing was needed in the church. How could these few diaconal ministers teach the denomination about diakonia? How could these few diaconal ministers make their voices heard?

The study group in 1980–1984 found itself between two opposing forces. One force was holding on to the Anglican/Roman tradition of a sequenced ordination from deacon to elder. The deacon identity was understood as part of the identity of the elder. This had been the practice of the Church of England in John Wesley's time and came across the Atlantic to the new Methodist movement. However, some Wesleyan groups did not adopt the practice. The Evangelical United Brethren had a single ordination for its elders. Mickle's 1982 article describes the confusion and ambiguity in the UMC surrounding diaconal ministry. The ecumenical dialogues were encouraging churches to form a permanent diaconate to address the needs of the world. The Anglican part of the Methodist tradition was opposed to discontinuing the current form of probationary deacon to create a distinctive deacon. Biblical scholarship was uncovering the meaning of *diakonia* and looking at how the early Christian community organized its leadership around certain tasks. While Acts 6 does not use the term *deacon,* the story reveals that the community identified and set aside some leaders for the work of charity, justice and Word.

The apostles lay hands on them and seem to authorize them for this specific work. All these issues were part of the context for the ministry discussions of GBHEM 1980–1984.

Mickle's *Quarterly Review* article summarizes the issues at stake for participants in the study. He urges consideration of them by the church because the diaconate could be a "means of church renewal" (Mickle, 59). He argued that a revised diaconal order would contribute to the church's mission as long as it was understood that "it is not intended to be a substitute for the *diakonia* of all Christians but rather is to be a representative of that *diakonia,* officially personifying Christ's ministry of service" (54). The Consultation on Church Union had proposed ordaining deacons to "struggle with the myriad needs of societies and persons in Christ's name, and so to exemplify the interdependence of worship and mssion in the life of the Church" (1985, 53). The COCU document also states that the diaconate "is a ministry in its own right and not a stepping-stone to other offices" (53).

Mickle also looked at the ordinal then in use by The United Methodist Church. He found that it incorporated much of the distinctive focus of *diakonia* into its language for the ordination of deacons who would "advance" to ordination as elders in as little as two years. The candidate for probationary deacon would be asked, "Will you, in the exercise of your ministry, represent to the people of God their own responsibility to serve others by an active concern for peace, justice, and freedom for all people?" (51). Mickle concludes, "For any who have eyes to see, it is clear that the 1980 ordinal for deacons has adopted the disciplinary provisions for diaconal ministry and has added them to the traditional functions of deacons. It is also evident that The United Methodist Church already had disciplinary provisions in its diaconal ministry for much of what COCU talks about in its 'Ministry of Deacons'" (52).

Mickle's theological rationale is that, while the church has always had leaders ordained to Word and sacrament, it would benefit missionally from leaders ordained to "Word and deed" (55). During this same quadrennium, according to Joaquin Garcia, theological clarity started emerging in some circles of the UMC regarding our belief in one baptism. There was no theological basis to support two ordinations, one for probationary members and one for elders. The group studying ministry found itself in the midst of rich theological dialogue, some coming from the ecumenical groups, and some simply in the larger dialogue.

Heitzenrater (1988, 8) is critical of the 1980–1984 study because he believes that too many participants in the dialogue were not theologically trained. As an historian of the Wesleyan movement, he advocated for faithfulness to that tradition. Bishops and other clergy who knew the tradition of the Roman and Anglican churches were best equipped to consider the ordering of ministry in the church, in his view. He reports that the commission passed a revised version "by a minority of 9 votes (out of 19; 4 absent, 3 abstaining, 3 against)" in 1983. The study committee was composed primarily of members from the three ministry divisions, but the Division of Ordained Ministry had less than one-third of the votes. That staff was strongly resisting the need for diaconal ministry in The United Methodist Church, but they could not control the outcome of the study.

The 1984 General Conference

Despite their resistance, the report to the 1984 General Conference proposed that the transitional deacon be eliminated; there should be one order of elder and one of deacon with full membership in the annual conference. Diaconal ordination would be to "Liturgy, Service, and Justice" (Daily Christian Advocate [DCA] 1984, 455). This change in terminology appears to reflect the broadening understanding of the deacon's call; the liturgical function of the order would keep the deacon closely tied to the church gathered as a worshiping congregation, and the justice call would keep the deacon's eye on the world and the need to move it closer to God's will.

The 1984 legislative committee, like the 1980 committee, continued to use the term *representative* to distinguish the ordained from the general ministry of all Christians. Heitzenrater (1988, 8), like other traditionalists, noted that *representative* "seems to mean everything and therefore nothing." However, the *Baptism, Eucharist, and Ministry* document from the World Council of Churches in 1982 had stated that "ordained ministers are representatives of Jesus Christ to the community, and proclaim his message of reconciliation" (21). The Ministry Study report and the General Conference legislative committee adopted the term that had come from the ecumenical dialogues.

The legislative committee of the 1984 General Conference voted nonconcurrence with the Ministry Study proposal, but the General Conference agreed by a two-thirds vote to suspend the rules and receive it as a minority report. Dr. E. Dale Dunlap, then dean at Saint Paul School of Theology and a Wesleyan scholar, was serving as a director of GBHEM and assigned to the Division of Ordained Ministry. Rena Yocom says that "though the division staff tried to silence (and some would say, shun) him, Dunlap would not let the call for the diaconate be ignored." During the General Conference plenary, Dunlap spoke. His summary claimed that the "special character of the ordained ministry consists precisely in its being an efficacious sign in the furtherance of the divine purpose, both in the church and in the world." The church needs "two non-hierarchical forms of representative ministry: one order of elder for the ministry of Word, sacrament, and order and one order of a permanent deacon for the ministry of liturgy, service, and justice" (DCA 1984, 455).

Rena Yocom and other diaconal ministers around the connection celebrated this strong statement from Dunlap; he had originally resisted the permanent deacon but had changed his mind and spoken out. Deaconess Kay Barckley (now a deacon) also spoke to the conference in favor of the report. She said, "The permanent diaconate will extend the ministry of our church towards the vision of what we are capable of doing to be in ministry and mission in the world. The church of the future must change its ministry to the changing needs of its members and churches" (DCA 1984, 458). However, the General Conference was not swayed by the speeches of Barckley or Dunlap and upheld the legislative committee's recommendation for nonconcurrence.

The 1984 General Conference then approved a Commission for the Study of Ministry for the next quadrennium. The charge this time was,

> [T]o conduct a broad and comprehensive study of the church's historic and contemporary theological understanding of ministry with specific emphasis on the meaning of ordination, the relation of ordination to the sacraments, the meaning of itineracy, and the nature of conference membership. It shall study the effectiveness of the church's present structure of ministry, consider the possibility of a permanent order of deacon, and recommend to the General Conference any necessary restructuring for effective ministry. It shall give appropriate consideration to all previous studies of ministry since 1968. (DCA 1984, 1209)

This time the conference asked for a commission to be named by the Council of Bishops. It should "include fair and adequate representation of the church geographically, ethnically, and shall include both female and male" (1210). It was to include five diaconal ministers along with five bishops, five faculty from seminaries, five elders, and ten laypersons. Given the criticism that earlier committees had included too many diaconal ministers and not enough theologically trained persons, this one was very heavy in the other direction. The bishops, seminary faculty, and elders made a group of fifteen. That left the laity and five diaconal ministers who might support the development of a permanent deacon.

The 1984–1988 Commission on the Study of Ministry

This quadrennium however, the study had official commission status. Instead of being the work of the General Board of Higher Education and Ministry, it was a duly authorized and independent commission, funded separately. Faith J. Conklin, an elder in the California-Pacific Conference serving as a district superintendent, was a member of the commission. She reported, in an article published in *Quarterly Review* in Spring 1988, that the commission had made "a decision to affirm a permanent ordained diaconate" (Conklin, 31). She also says that it was a consensus decision; she is one of those who changed her mind about the issue because of the commission's work. The consensus was that the deacon and elder in this new ordering would be collegial and not competitive. Her words confirm this shift:

> Their ministries are not mutually exclusive. In their unity they represent the essential wholeness of the church's ministry. In their differences they are a visible reminder of the diversity of the Spirit's gifts for ministry. Similarly, the tasks of the deacon and the elder are complementary. Deacon and elder share some essential tasks, such as teaching, proclamation, education, nurture, and liturgical responsibilities, but each brings a different or distinctive focus to the exercise of that task (32).

Conklin resisted the easy definition by function that plagues the deacon to the present. This description of the overlap but the distinctiveness of focus is difficult for some who want to define each order in relationship to its authorization (or lack of authorization) for presiding at the sacraments.

As a deacon myself, whose ministry has often overlapped my elder colleagues, I claim that distinctive focus. The work of this commission produced a nuanced and well-articulated rationale for two orders of ordained clergy: deacon and elder. The church needs the elder to order the church, preach the Word, and offer the sacraments. The church needs deacons to lead and equip the laity for their mission. These orders should be distinct and complementary, but not hierarchical.

Conklin also names the big stumbling block to the acceptance of the recommendations from this commission: "It will be difficult to dislodge our deeply ingrained notion that the Order of Deacon is a temporary station on the way to higher and better things, the Order of Elder" (36). Conklin was quoting Bishop Boulton, but this deeply ingrained notion is still present forty years later. Too often, deacons are asked when they will become a *real* minister. The term denotes, for some, an incomplete status. Some United Methodists still think of the deacon as a transitional and temporary state where the church examines candidates for ordination as elders. Another stumbling block then and now is that some deacons remain who are local pastors; they have completed the Course of Study and have been elected as associate members of the annual conference. Also confusing the picture both then and now is the deaconess, which is a lay office.

Conklin also takes on the issue of itineracy, which had been required of elders beginning with Francis Asbury's superintendency. Because ordination required a candidate to agree to itinerate at the request of the resident bishop, the denomination had great flexibility and could put ordained leaders in most any context that served the mission. Boards of Ordained Ministry and bishops continue to ask to this day, will you go where you are sent? Some elders have willingly submitted to itinerate, but we do not actually have a fully itinerant ministry. The needs of families and spouses must be considered, so some elders cannot move to just any appointment. Some elders are in *extension* ministries: conference or agency staff, faculty of a seminary or college, or chaplaincy positions responsible to an agency outside the UMC where itineration makes no sense. As the church has grown more diverse, attention to race, language, culture, gender, ethnicity, and gifts of the elder affect her or his ability to itinerate. Deacons would not be part of the itineration in the same way. As Conklin wrote, "A non-itinerating deacon may free the church to consider alternative forms for its mission" (Conklin 1988, 39).

The 1988 Study of Ministry Commission envisioned an ordained permanent deacon that is similar to the concept accepted in 1996. But it did not offer any legislation to make it a reality. Instead, it requested that the study continue for another four years. The commission rightly identified one reason that the same questions had been considered and the same recommendations had been brought to General Conferences since 1968: each study group begins over. No mechanism exists for it to build on what has come before because it has always been a whole new group of people who have not come to a consensus. Their report asked for four more years for the same group.

Not surprisingly, many of those who resisted the formation of a permanent diaconate did not approve. "I would say that this maneuver is the result of the negative reaction from around the church to yet another report that essentially starts and ends at the same places as the last two reports that have both been rejected by the General Conference" (Heitzenrater, 1988, 9). The Council of Bishops commended the commission for its work but offered an alternative that would continue only one-third of those who had served on the 1984–1988 study.

The 1988 General Conference

In 1988, Mary Elizabeth Moore, a diaconal minister and faculty member at Claremont School of Theology, was a jurisdictional delegate and attended General Conference to support the legislative committee working on the ministry section of the *Discipline*. She came to it with deep experience of both theological and practical issues around ministry. After careful discernment, she had been convinced that she was called to this new ministry, and she was consecrated in 1977. She was asked to chair the new California–Pacific Conference Board of Diaconal Ministry in 1978 and remained in that position for eight years. She had many conversations about this new form of ministry. She became convinced that diaconal ministry was not fully formed; she recalls doing "tons of research."

The research contributed to Moore's work as the primary writer for *Called to Serve: The United Methodist Diaconate*, published by GBHEM in 1987. Also contributing to the book were historian Rosemary Skinner Keller and Gerald F. Moede, an experienced participant in the ecumenical dialogues. In the process of writing *Called to Serve*, Moore was struck by the significance of the diaconate in the early church and the political resistance that accompanied it. In Orthodox churches, the diaconate did not go away, but in Western Christianity it eventually disappeared except for the deaconess movement. Following World War II, the notion of *diakonia* experienced a resurgence, especially in the Episcopal Church and the United Church of Canada. The Roman Catholic Church had also begun to train and ordain deacons. *Called to Serve* told all of this story.

Another issue for Moore was her observation that diaconal ministers (mostly employed by local churches) were having a difficult time; they were often not treated fairly in employment or offered insurance or other benefits. The way the church defined *elder* was too narrow to fully address its mission, she believed. "The elder seeks to connect with the world, but we need ministries grounded in the world," she asserts. She longed for the day when the missional significance of *diakonia* would be recognized in The United Methodist Church.

As the 1988 legislative committee responsible for the ministry study and other legislation related to ministry began its work, Dr. Moore was alert to ways she could offer insight and advice to the delegates related to diaconal ministry: "The chair and vice chair led the group carefully toward a certain end. There was little discussion and a lot of confusion." Moore remembers how little support there was in the legislative committee: "The issue of diaconate was raised but the discussion was all toward rejection. The largest resistance was that it would confuse the elder and move us away from the historic [Anglican, Catholic, Episcopal] orders of ministry." The legislative committee voted nonconcurrence.

When the Ministry Study Commission report came to the floor of the 1988 General Conference, the debate revealed the usual squabbling. The arguments supporting the long-time traditions of the church were present. The arguments that the times call for a new ordained leader, focused on mission in the world were also there. As Heitzenrater (1988, 12) observed, "Nearly everything is up for grabs every four years at General Conference." The 1984–1988 commission included very few scholars, which gave the General Conference one reason to look askance. Rena Yocom, who had served as secretary for the commission, remembers a "very verbal put down." Consideration of the report got bogged down in multiple amendments to the make-up of the recommended commission for 1988–1992. Instead of continuing the same group, the decision was that half of the 1984–88 group could continue (to be chosen by the Council of Bishops) and half would be new.

As Ruth Daugherty, who had chaired the commission, pointed out, with that much change of membership in the next quadrennium she "could not even begin to say what the contents of that will be" (DCA, 1988, 478). One delegate's speech expressed frustration that the commission did not complete its work but instead asked to be continued. Clark said, "We have given a mandate in 1984 that this commission was to bring back a study. . . . Now, what is the accountability of this commission to us not having done that?" (479). The report prevailed with a vote of 583 yes, 373 no. However, the teeth had been taken out of its recommendations because the request to continue the commission membership was diluted to half.

The Ecumenical Community Supports the Deacon

During the 1980s, the ecumenical community was responding to *Baptism, Eucharist, and Ministry* (*BEM*). The World Council of Churches first published the document in 1982, but versions had been under discussion since 1927 by its Faith and Order Commission. The three essential areas for which they sought unity were reflected in the title: baptism, eucharist, and ministry. Rena Yocom had been elected as a national director for the National Council of Churches (NCC) in 1980. The NCC was also seeking ecumenical dialogue and unity. Yocom served the NCC as vice president (1986–1989) and chaired their committee on faith and order. She had rich experience with the issues related to the dialogue. When *Baptism, Eucharist, and Ministry* was passed at the World Council, the United Methodist bishops asked for a committee to draft the United Methodist response. Yocom was named to that committee and, in fact, was one of the drafters of the ministry response section for the UMC. She recalls that there really wasn't any solid agreement with the ministry section of *BEM* from either the National Council of Churches or the UMC. At NCC, the free church people "didn't buy into the ministry section at all." The Presbyterians could not support the section on bishops. *BEM* had picked up the permanent diaconate because they were, in some ways, a reflection from Vatican II. "There were parts that we really wanted to affirm but even the Methodists didn't really go along with the three orders because our bishops are not a separate order. I was in the midst of it," says Yocom. So Yocom was at the center of the ecumenical dialogues as a director of the National Council of Churches and part of the United Methodist Faith and Order Commission for twelve years. She had served on the 1984–1988 Ministry Study Commission too.

In 1988, the efforts to promote a permanent deacon for the UMC appeared stalled. Two ministry studies had proposed a renewed form of diaconate for the church. However, the General Conference seemed not to take the proposals seriously in 1984 or 1988. But the idea was continuing to mature in a variety of ways, particularly due to the excellent and expansive leadership of the Division of Diaconal Ministry staff. The history of the UMC reveals that any social change takes time. The church needs to hear a new idea repeatedly before it is ready to accept it. For instance, in predecessor denominations, the idea of ordaining women took nearly a century! And the notion that women could be bishops also took another twenty years to come to fruition.

Joaquin Garcia recalls that Bishop David Frederick Wertz spoke these words at a meeting of the Division of Diaconal Ministry, "We should join the parade and not let the parade pass us by." The parade was definitely forming in support of an ordained deacon to lead the diaconal ministry of the UMC, but it was not quite moving down the road to approval yet.

4 The Collective Groan in 1992

The Almost Deacon

This quadrennium (1988–1992) brought the United Methodist permanent diaconate to the brink of redefinition as an ordained deacon. The project was moving on several fronts: through the direct work of the GBHEM staff, through the legislative proposals from the Study of Ministry Commission, and through growth in the visibility of diaconal ministry throughout the church. All of it came to a dramatic climax on the evening of May 15, 1992 in General Conference action.

The Work of GBHEM, 1988–1992

In November 1991, GBHEM published an Occasional Paper written by Rosalie Bentzinger, "Putting an End to the Confusion: A Renewed Order of Deacon." She began with a rebuke to those who were asking, "What do diaconal ministers want?" She wrote, "It is a frequently asked question, but it does not strike at the heart of the matter." Instead, Bentzinger identified the real questions: "What does the church need in order to be faithful to its call to continue Christ's ministry? What structures enable persons to be in ministry and which block and impede their serving?" (1991, 1).

GBHEM leadership and staff were all working to help create structures that would support the church's mission and ministry. So were *some* of those who were elected directors of the GBHEM Board. And, although the consecrated diaconal ministers knew that they were officially laypersons, they also knew that their identity was much more like clergy. They felt like neither fish nor fowl, officially laity but more like clergy in their self-understanding, not really fitting in either category. They knew for sure they had been called and made a lifetime commitment to serve the church as part of its leadership.

Although the 1988 Ministry Study Commission report had articulated a rich understanding of how a new office of permanent ordained deacon would contribute to the church's mission, it garnered very little support at that General Conference. However, things at the General Board of Higher Education and Ministry were about to evolve. Trotter retired and Dr. Roger Ireson was elected as general secretary in 1988. He would remain in that position until 2001. He describes the tension between the two divisions—Diaconal Ministry and Ordained Ministry—as "tremendous" when he arrived. When Ireson arrived, Rosalie Bentzinger was associate general secretary of the Division of Diaconal Ministry and Don Treece was associate general secretary of the Division of Ordained Ministry. Bentzinger and Treece were on opposite sides of issues relating to an ordained diaconate. The members of the 1984–1988 Commission on the Study of Ministry felt disappointed at the lack of support for their work too. The Division of Diaconal Ministry was relieved that the new general secretary seemed open to the idea of a stronger diaconate. "I felt strongly as general secretary that the deacon should be ordained, not only an order, because it could easily become a second-tier ministry," Ireson recalls.

Bentzinger's staff had expanded. Joaquin Garcia, hired nearly ten years before (1979), was working with conference relations, helping annual conference Boards of Diaconal Ministry to hold to denominational standards and identify good candidates for consecration as diaconal ministers. He also administered the church-related certification programs. Paul Van Buren joined the division in 1985. His area of responsibility was professional development, which included standards, professional organizations, and seminary relations. He was also leading in the development of new forms of diaconal/deacon ministries. The three of them provided visibility and leadership for diaconal ministry.

One of the concerning trends in the population of diaconal ministers was that it was overwhelmingly female and white. Paul Van Buren was asked to take on a research project that sought "to hear the voices of the ethnic population in The United Methodist Church of North America on particular needs, and to enable those voices to be heard" (Division of Diaconal Ministry, *Needs*

Assessment of Ethnic Minority Churches and Communities for Specialized Ministries [Nashville, 1989], acknowledgments). This was a massive project, and Van Buren partnered with Dr. Daniel B. Lee, a diaconal minister who was associate professor of Social Work at The Ohio State University.

Their research discovered multiple needs in these communities that diaconal ministers could address as well as the constraints that were limiting the use of diaconal ministers. Not surprisingly, economics were often cited, but they also found little understanding of diaconal ministry by laity or senior pastors in the ethnic communities. They urged a broadening of the image of diaconal ministry, adopting innovative approaches to the ministerial preparation of persons who would serve ethnic communities, and creating "tent-making" or self-supporting ministries. More candidates for diaconal ministry from minority communities needed to be recruited and supported. Of course, they said little about the challenges that most of the White, middle-class women who were diaconal ministers would encounter in entering another culture and another ethnic setting. Lee and Van Buren's research was funded by the Division of Diaconal Ministry and its Ethnic Concerns Committee. The issues that come to light in this report remain present today, more than thirty years later. The study exhibits the commitment of the division to increasing the diversity of diaconal ministers and the places they served, but the mission suggested by the research has not yet been fully realized.

Meanwhile the staff of GBHEM was busy with a new task. The 1988 General Conference had approved an ambitious new project to start a university on the African continent. General Secretary Trotter had worked hard to be sure that GBHEM would take the lead in establishing Africa University. When Roger Ireson was elected general secretary, he inherited this responsibility. The Division of Higher Education staff had responsibility for United Methodist colleges, universities, and seminaries. Some expected that they would be the ones to work on Africa University. But Ireson decided not to limit it. "I decided for the Africa University project that we would use our entire staff. That included the diaconal staff too," he recalls. Ireson's decision had implications for the acceptance and development of the deacon.

Rosalie Bentzinger worked with the committee to design the College of Education for the new university, a field in which she held a graduate degree. The goal was to prepare teachers for African school systems. Bentzinger told a newspaper reporter that she made five trips to Africa and "worked with a committee of a dozen persons from six African countries and the U. S. They are all highly educated and although they speak either French, English, or Portuguese, we communicate with some help from able interpreters" (Randolph 2014).

Paul Van Buren had served as a missionary in the Philippines and was completing a doctorate in agriculture at Ohio State University. He was chairing the Board of Diaconal Ministry in the East Ohio Conference when he was hired at GBHEM in 1985. He also had a Master of Christian Education degree from Methodist Theological School of Ohio. So, his academic credentials were strong, and Ireson used him extensively in the beginning stages of establishing Africa University. This meant that highly educated and competent diaconal ministers became visible in a variety of settings, a corrective to the dominant image of diaconal ministers as undereducated women working with children.

Bentzinger also assigned Van Buren to give attention to emerging ministries that expanded diaconal ministry beyond Christian education and other congregational staff settings. The focus of diaconal ministry was defined as "love, service, justice," which could encompass many specialized ministry settings in the world as well as in the church. Although the first step toward a permanent diaconate in the UMC was professional certification for those who would work in the church, both the lay worker of 1968 and the diaconal minister of 1976 were more generalized. The Disciplinary language of love, service, and justice (1976, ¶301) was intended to capture a broader understanding rather than naming specific professions such as youth ministry. Van Buren began meeting with seminaries to encourage them to find ways to equip persons called to these new diaconal ministries through either certification studies or masters degrees.

Van Buren says, "Hiring me was an interesting gamble. I was an anomaly, with my scientific background in agriculture." Yet, he provided a wonderful model for a broadening concept of how diaconal ministers might serve the broader mission of the church. The 1988 *Discipline* states, "Diaconal ministers focus their service through a variety of ministries, such as, administration, education, evangelism, music, health ministries, and community development—to the local congregation and the wider community. . . . Diaconal ministry exists to intensify and make more effective the self-understanding of the whole people of God as servants in Christ's name" (¶109). This provided Van Buren with a clear directive to expand the range of ministries appropriate for diaconal ministers. In between his trips to Africa

University and meetings related to it, he was teaching the church to enlarge its vision of the diaconate.

The Division of Diaconal Ministry was also making good progress in establishing a Board of Diaconal Ministry in every US conference and setting standards for their work. Under the guidance of Joaquin Garcia, *A Candidacy Journal* was published and in use to guide the discernment process for candidates. In 1988, a set of guidelines for the psychological assessment of candidates was ready for use by conference boards. The General Board of Finance and Administration (GCFA) came on board with a fund in which diaconal ministers could invest and save toward retirement. Also in 1988, the third edition of *The Christian as Minister*, a resource for persons who think that they may be called to ministry, was published. This time, Joaquin Garcia was a member of the editorial committee, ensuring that the distinctive call and identity of diaconal ministers was presented as one of the options. Diaconal ministry had not been fully included in the first or second editions, so including it in 1988 represented a step toward equal status with elders. Diaconal ministers were establishing a more secure place in the church where their ministries could thrive.

Each Conference Board of Diaconal Ministry was encouraged to attend its jurisdictional training event. Garcia recalls that the staff of the division was intentionally building a cadre of mutual support in each conference. Together, they were developing some common language to interpret diaconal ministry and professional certification: "The concept was for the local churches and annual conferences to recognize God's call to persons who would lead ministries of love, service, and justice, and to equip the church to serve the community and the world. Doing this led into greater awareness of the uniqueness of call and response, and how equipping, fulfilling the personal, theological, educational, and church requirements, and areas of specialized ministry could be developed."

Publication of pamphlets, journal articles, and handbooks was prioritized by the GBHEM staff. *Called to Serve: The United Methodist Diaconate* by Dr. Mary Elizabeth Moore, Dr. Rosemary Skinner Keller, and Gerald F. Moede, was published in 1987 by the Division of Diaconal Ministry. The book put forth a theological, historical, ecumenical, and biblical view of the diaconate by a formidable trio of writers. Keller was a historian with academic credentials, Moede had been part of ecumenical dialogues for many years, and Moore was a diaconal minister and scholar of practical theology with experience at the conference and general church level. The book is comprehensive and scholarly.

The Division of Diaconal Ministry hoped that bishops, General Conference delegates, diaconal ministers, and other leaders would read it. The authors argue that The United Methodist Church needs to move "beyond the idea of diaconal ministry simply as an umbrella for various lay ministries that have been in existence." In addition, the authors urge keeping "the focus on the purposes and meaning of ministry rather than on the balance of power and recognition" between elders and diaconal ministers. They also reiterate that liturgy and service cannot be separated: "The unity of worship and service in the church and world [must be] symbolized and enabled" (73). Then they write, "United Methodists believe that it is theologically important to symbolize and embody the unity of the church in the ministry of the bishop and to symbolize and embody the priestly ministry of the church in the ministry of the elder/priest. If we are consistent, we need likewise to consider the value of symbolizing and embodying the *servanthood* of the church in the ministry of the deacon" (74).

The Division of Diaconal Ministry, with the help of diaconal ministers and conference boards, was slowly building awareness of the distinctive call to love, service, and justice, as well as the range of ministries that this call might address. By creating the lay worker in 1968, the General Conference had sought to recognize professionals working in the church and find ways to both safeguard their employment and include them in conference structures. Twenty years later (1988–1992), the lay worker had evolved into the diaconal minister, which was more clearly defined with expanded boundaries. Rather than being a place for church professionals, the church had affirmed the need for a gifted and called vocation that was situated in some specialized ministries. In addition, diaconal ministry provided a place for persons working in a variety of ministries beyond the church who would be clearly connected back to the conference and the worshiping congregation.

This expanded conception built on the notion that all Christians are called to ministry by their baptism. And some are called to representative ministry that equips the people of God for their ministry in the world. In twenty years, diaconal ministry had grown into an office that paralleled the elder in its rigorous discernment process for candidates and its high standards for those who would be consecrated. The staff of GBHEM and their partners across the church had built something that was contributing in meaningful ways to the mission of The United Methodist Church.

The Ministry Study Commission Report in 1992

In the background of the 1988–1992 Commission for the Study of Ministry was the work of the Consultation on Church Union (COCU). The ecumenical work of this organization of churches in the United States had produced a document in 1985 that was helpful for the 1988 study commission's report. The concept of a permanent deacon with a distinctive role of service and liturgy quoted earlier, which the 1988 group articulated, was very much in harmony with the COCU work. COCU declared,

> Deacons are baptized members of the People of God, ordained to represent to the People its identity in Christ as a body of persons who are in service both to Church and world. It belongs to diaconal ministry to struggle with the myriad needs of societies and persons in Christ's name, and so to exemplify the interdependence of worship and mission in the life of the Church (COCU 1985, 52–53).

With this strong statement of support for an ordained deacon coming from the COCU dialogue, the new Ministry Study Commission began its work in 1988. However, Yocom reports that "the most frequent charge against the '88 Report was that it was 'not Wesleyan.' It often came [camouflaged] as a charge of being too influenced by the ecumenical movement" (1991, 127). The General Conference of 1988 asked the new Ministry Study Commission to continue the discussion about ordained and diaconal ministry, but it specified that the membership would be appointed by the Council of Bishops and would move well beyond the GBHEM folks who had been the majority on previous commissions. This new commission had thirty-five members. Not surprisingly, the study came to a different conclusion. Its recommendation was that the diaconal minister be replaced with a consecrated lay order of deacon.

The Commission Report to the 1992 General Conference

The 1988–1992 Ministry Study Commission had been directed to send its report to the 1992 General Conference through the Council of Bishops. The

Council was not in agreement with the report and sent a petition to the 1992 General Conference asking that the whole matter be referred back to the Council of Bishops. This could effectively make the commission's work moot.

When Bishop Grove called the General Conference to order on the afternoon of May 15, 1992, that petition from the Council of Bishops was before them. Before any action on that item, Ruth Daugherty, a lay delegate from Eastern Pennsylvania, chair of the Ministry Study Commission, was invited to present a report of the commission's work. As the commission was acting in response to the last General Conference, they agreed to hear its report even though they were about to vote on referral, a tactic that, essentially, would kill its proposals. Daugherty described the commission as "representative of the diversity and the inclusiveness of this church," clearly alluding to a criticism of the 1984–1988 Study Commission. She named the three principles that guided their work: a missional focus, the call to service of all baptized Christians, and the ecumenical consensus that there are three distinct ministries (deacon, elder, and bishop). The commission recommended a permanent lay order of deacon with responsibility "to initiate their service assignments," but left the final authority to the bishop "to approve or not approve those service assignments" (DCA 1992, 647).[1] They also recommended a single ordination for elders to Word, sacrament, and order. Daugherty stressed the commission's efforts to seek the will of the church and the strong consensus around the commission's report. The presiding bishop, Bishop Grove, then explained to the conference that the commission's work was assigned to the legislative committee. At that point, it became the property of the legislative committee and could be changed. Then they adjourned for dinner.

The General Conference Receives the Legislative Committee Recommendation: The Near Miss

Following the break, Bishop Grove moved to the report of the legislative committee on Ordained and Diaconal Ministry. The chair was Dr. Dennis Campbell, dean of the Divinity School at Duke University. The secretary was Mary Elizabeth Moore, then a professor at Claremont School of Theology. Moore was an expert on the history of the diaconate in Christianity and co-author of *Called to Serve*, which had been published the previous year. However, when she was elected as secretary of the legislative committee, she found that her voice was muted. The chair controlled the discussion and did not allow the officers to speak.

Linda Marshall, a diaconal minister delegate and a member of that legislative committee, was frustrated. She recalls that Moore "was silenced during the legislative session, she was not allowed to speak. So much of what she could have shared would have saved us so much time. That was an eye-opening experience in my naïve world." Moore, along with Linda Marshall and others from the legislative committee were on the platform when the report began. They had asked if they should get a reserve from their delegations to be seated in case a vote was taken and Campbell had said no. So no one could vote in their place. This would essentially disenfranchise them and prove to be important when the issues finally came to a vote.

The legislative committee first considered the petition from the Council of Bishops to refer the commission's recommendations for more study. Campbell stated that "it was the judgment of the committee that decision and action, not referral, was in order." The committee recommended nonconcurrence with the Council of Bishop's request. The conference voted to table the bishops' petition. This created a legislative space for the body to hear the report from the legislative committee.

Campbell then moved into the primary proposals coming from the legislative committee. He testified that "the committee worked long hours and labored diligently. I want to emphasize long hours" (DCA 1992, 650). The days in that committee room must have been very intense. Mary Elizabeth Moore recalls that it was "hotly debated." Jack Harnish, an elder from Michigan who would join the staff of GBHEM in 1993, calls it a "heated debate." Another of the delegates, who argued strongly against the creation of a permanent ordained deacon, was Jerome King Del Pino, clergy from New England. However, more and more delegates to the General Conference, along with other United Methodists, were becoming convinced that an ordained deacon would better serve the mission of the church. Many United Methodists in Louisville for the conference followed the progress of petitions assigned to this committee eagerly. It must have been exhausting for all who served on that legislative committee.

When their report came up on the plenary agenda, some in the convention hall were quite anxious. Issues related to the topic had been debated at every General Conference since the beginning of the denomination. The air in the convention center was charged that night. Diaconal ministers were holding their breath and hoping that the proposals would pass.

Campbell first offered what he called "3 key petitions" that represented the crux of the committee's work. The first was "to create a new order of deacon to take the place of what we now call 'diaconal ministers.' This would be an *ordained* order of deacon. The deacons would be full clergy members of the annual conference, ordained to liturgy and service." This was quite a change from the consecrated *lay* deacon the ministry study had proposed earlier. The legislative committee proposed a permanent ordained deacon with membership in the annual conference. The second key proposal eliminated the transitional ordination to deacon for those seeking to become elders. This was probably the most controversial petition. The third key proposal would deal with membership in the annual conference.

The debate began. Some delegates were prepared to speak in favor. Others were prepared to speak against, hoping to preserve the status quo. Doris J. Rudy, lay leader from Northern Illinois Conference, urged the General Conference to concur with the legislative committee. This was an important voice. Rudy was a mover and shaker among the lay leaders. She urged acceptance of a new deacon, ordained to liturgy and service. Part of her argument was that a "consecrated lay deacon might create an undesirable gradation of laity" (DCA 1992, 651). As long as diaconal ministers or a consecrated lay deacon remained defined as a part of the lay representation in conferences, some laity felt that they were losing their voice.

Speeches against the proposal were made by several elders who made the argument that the issues needed more study, that deleting sequential ordination of elders would break with tradition, and that ordination should be limited to the traditional priestly ministries of Word, sacrament, and order. They also made a passionate appeal to maintain the itineracy; they argued that those who were ordained in Methodism had always agreed to be sent on behalf of the mission of the church. "I submit that itinerancy is not as the majority proposal assumes, merely a thing indifferent, an administrative baggage that we can now discard for the sake of the creation of this new order. This is what is at stake in the decision you will make," proclaimed Lawrence McCleskey, clergy from Western North Carolina (DCA 1992, 651).

Quite a bit of time was spent in clarifying what decisions were before the conference and then the discussion turned to "liturgy and service," which had been named as the identifiers of the new order. Moore, finally allowed to speak, was asked to clarify those terms. She spoke from her research about the historical role of the deacon and explained to the conference that those two words,

> go deep into the history of the Christian church. The early church had bishops, presbyters, and deacons. The deacon's role was a ministry of liturgy and service. The role was to assist the presbyter and bishop in the worship and to lead the community in acts of service in the world. . . . It is a role that deacons do because they are especially called to give leadership to the church in liturgy and service (DCA 1992, 654).

Later in the debate, she had the opportunity to assert that "In the Roman Catholic, Greek Orthodox, Episcopal, and Presbyterian churches, for example, deacons are ordained as permanent deacons" (655).

After more parliamentary maneuvering, Rev. Kelly Bender, chair of the Kansas East Board of Ordained Ministry, spoke in favor of the legislative committee proposal. This is the same conference where Rena Yocom was located, so he probably had a tutor and had heard the history of these considerations. He said,

> To suggest that the legislative committee recommendation has somehow emerged without foresight and care is unwarranted. It is an outgrowth of 20 years of dialogue, reflection, and discernment within The United Methodist Church and the ecumenical church. I believe the Holy Spirit has been present and participant in the legislative committee recommendation. I believe the recommendation reflects a clear, consistent theology of ordination; a clear, consistent structuring of ministry. And I believe it will empower ministry. (656)

The debate continued for quite a while with questions about whether these deacons would qualify for pensions, housing, and so on. Perhaps these questions expressed genuine confusion, and perhaps they were intended to raise anxiety among the delegates who might vote for the proposal. Linda Marshall, then a diaconal minister, was on the platform for the report. She remembers:

> When questions were asked, Dennis would have this kind of chaotic response and he would flail his arms and would look around as if, is there anybody who could answer this? Here was Mary Elizabeth ready to answer and he would just keep moving on and try to bumble his way through the answer. It was a very effective method.

Marshall feels that Campbell "made it sound like we didn't have a clue what was going on. Mary Elizabeth Moore could have carefully answered and dispelled all the anxiety. That was my first true experience of being totally silenced and in despair."

Ultimately, the question put to a vote was an amendment to delete the words "by ordination" and "for the ministry of liturgy and service" from line 3 in calendar item 1219. A yes vote would essentially overturn the recommendation from the legislative committee. The vote was 480 yes and 478 no. According to Mary Elizabeth Moore, When the vote was announced, "there was a collective groan. Because General Conference doesn't normally have such close decisions. A close decision tells you something about the church. There was a collective groan." The establishment of a permanent ordained deacon failed by two votes in 1988.

Those who had favored the new ordained deacon were disappointed and angry. Linda Marshall recalls that she was in despair after that vote. She was ready to "totally quit!" The proposal failed by only two votes, but more than two delegates were on the platform who would have voted yes. They could not vote from the platform, which was not in the bar of the conference. Barbara Blackstone from Western Pennsylvania raised the question a bit later. "We have so many of the people who are most eligible in the whole house who are sitting on the platform. Could they not come to the floor too, so that they are not disenfranchised?" (660). But the vote stood. The motion to refer it to the Council of Bishops was brought off the table and the whole matter was referred to the Council of Bishops for the next quadrennium.

A Collective Groan Means Four More Years without Resolution

According to General Secretary Roger Ireson, the response of many diaconal ministers around the connection was intense: "That was felt very, very deeply. After the General Conference of 1992, I had diaconals crying everywhere. They were coming to us. They were in tears. They felt that once again they had been put down by the church. Their ministry had not been recognized or validated by the church." It was so disappointing to get within two votes of their goal. Many diaconal ministers were convinced that ordination would enhance their ministry and further the mission of the church.

Ecumenical guidelines and publications were helpful, but not enough to advance the permanent *diakonia* in The United Methodist Church. The staff at GBHEM was learning a lot about how to present options to the General Conference that were more likely to achieve the desired outcome. Joaquin Garcia remembers, "We learned some very important lessons. When you send a petition to General Conference that affects a paragraph of the *Book of Discipline*, it is open for discussion, additions, and amendments, and the outcome can be completely different from the original petition. In addition, we learned that the selection of the presiding bishop in each session matters and the calendar committee determined what items were going to be brought up during the plenary session. All of this was extremely important." Each time elections were held for delegates to General Conference, any diaconal ministers who were elected were encouraged to organize and be ready to speak to the issues. In 1992, Jimmy Carr, a diaconal minister serving in Mississippi, was one of the key persons in the network to shepherd the legislation relating to diaconal ministry. In the next quadrennium, Carr joined the staff of GBHEM as associate general secretary.

Despite the Groan, the UMC Moves Ahead

The United Methodist Church was creating a more fully developed theology of its mission and ministry in the decades from 1984 to 2004. *The United Methodist Hymnal* was approved by the 1988 General Conference and published in 1989. Its preface states that "much care has been taken to provide hymns and prayers from our rich ethnic diversity" and "its content reflects our Wesleyan heritage and witness: evangelical and ecumenical." Hymnals have always been important for Methodists as expressions that both form and inform faith. Those who sing their faith find the tunes and poetry circulating in their memory with power. This hymnal was careful to include a diverse set of images for God and a strong theology of mission. It has shaped the denomination to this day. A *Book of Worship* (1992) that provides liturgies and services also helps form the theology of United Methodists. Documents expressing United Methodist theology related to baptism (*By Water and the Spirit*, 1996) and Holy Communion (*This Holy Mystery*, 2004) have since been adopted by General Conferences. The new denomination has slowly articulated its doctrine, always honoring its Wesleyan heritage but also attending to its practical tasks in the moment. In 1992, when the divided

General Conference referred the question about a permanent deacon to the Council of Bishops, the denomination was being formed by its hymns, its vision of a university for the African continent, and its zeal to grow disciples through disciplined Bible study along with liturgical practices developed by a melding of tradition and contemporary values.

Rena Yocom had been shaped by not only that denominational culture but also her extensive work on both United Methodist ministry studies and on the Faith and Order Commission of the National Council of Churches. In 1991, she completed a project that earned her a Doctor of Ministry degree at San Francisco Theological Seminary. *In Diakonia* is a study of the history of *diakonia* from the sources in the New Testament to the present. She explored the issue using the guidelines of Scripture, experience, reason, and tradition. Her knowledge of the roots and possibilities of *diakonia* had come a long way since she asked the heartfelt question of the Commission for the Study of Ministry in 1972, "Is there no ecclesial affirmation for my call?" The doctoral project was informed by her participation in Ministry Study Commissions and the Division of Diaconal Ministry. She also contributed to the United Methodist response to *Baptism, Eucharist, and Ministry*, the statement from the World Council of Churches Commission on Faith and Order. She had participated in dialogues at the highest level. She was well-qualified to write *In Diakonia*, which became a resource for the ministry study 1992–1996.

The experiences of the 1992 General Conference were important. Those who believed that a permanent ordained deacon would advance the mission of the church in the world had learned some important lessons about the legislative process. They had found a lot of support among lay delegates, and some elders had seen the value of their proposal. These allies were critical. In addition, they understood how vital the selection of officers for the legislative committee could be. They realized that they needed to work with the agenda committee to put their legislation in a good place for fruitful debate. And they knew that they needed to talk with delegates ahead of time to help them see the possibilities of the deacon. They also knew the arguments that would come from delegates who loved the traditions and would resist giving them up. Mary Elizabeth Moore and other diaconal ministers who would write the petitions in 1996 were determined to be better prepared.

5 Setting the Stage
From 1992 to the
1996 General Conference

The 1992–1996 quadrennium began with diaconal ministers discouraged and angry. Many believed that the church had not affirmed their call to a lifetime, set-apart ministry. They also were convinced that the church needed ordained deacons whose ministry would lead and equip the people of God for their mission in the world. Deacons would *complement* the ministry of elders; their ministry would be different but not subservient. Thus, the transitional practice of ordaining those on the elder track as deacons would need to stop. Others in the church were deeply committed to the historical practices that came from the Anglican/Roman tradition of a priestly office with sequential ordination. They argued that the elder too was seeking justice and concerned about the world, which, of course, was true. After the close decision of the 1992 General Conference, the consideration of the forms of ordained ministry needed in The United Methodist Church was sent back to the Council of Bishops, yet again! The tension was unresolved. Both sides were passionate.

This chapter will describe some of the ways that the GBHEM staff and board continued to spread the word about the ministry being led by diaconal ministers. They also continued to press for high standards for candidates seeking to become diaconal ministers and made the standards parallel to those for elders. They sponsored the first of several Mission Caravans; this one was a peace caravan to Sarajevo. Meanwhile, at least one group of diaconal ministers took on the task of circulating a newsletter that continued the dialogue about ministry issues. The Division of Diaconal Ministry sponsored a national convocation, which attracted many diaconal ministers. It occurred just as the Council of Bishops was releasing their ministry report for the 1996 General Conference. The diaconal ministers at the convocation were not satisfied with conclusions of the new ministry study, and so they formed a small "clearness committee" to write legislation that would offer revisions. During this quadrennium, enhanced scholarship emerged related to the diaconate; diaconal ministers became more involved and skilled in political activity. All the while, the Council of Bishops was preparing to offer a proposal for re-ordering ministry.

Diaconal Ministers and GBHEM Staff Prepare for 1996

The original impetus that led to diaconal ministry had come from efforts to make a place for professionals—mostly musicians and Christian educators but others, such as pastoral counselors—employed by the church. By 1992, its focus had expanded; diaconal ministers were called and set apart for ministries of love, service, and justice. Some continued to specialize in worship and music or Christian education, but they had come to understand that their ultimate task was leading and equipping all the people of God for their ministries in the world. In the 1992 *Book of Discipline,* ¶103 is located in a section labeled "The Ministry of all Christians." It states, "As servants of Christ we are sent into the world to engage in the struggle for justice and reconciliation. We seek to reveal the love of God for men, women, and children of all ethnic, racial, cultural, and national backgrounds and to demonstrate the healing power of the gospel with those who suffer." The theological understanding of mission clearly pointed to work in the world. Diaconal ministers were claiming a self-understanding that embraced the connection to the work of justice and reconciliation.

In 1976, when diaconal ministry was established, its chapter required only five pages in the *Discipline.* By 1992, the section had expanded to thirteen pages, indicating the clarification of standards and processes as well as the expanded identity. Perhaps the primary sentences come in ¶301: "This set-apart ministry is not a substitute for the diaconal responsibility of all members of the general ministry. Rather, it exists to intensify and make more effective the self-understanding of the whole People of God as servants in Christ's name." This statement first appeared in 1980. It directly addressed the concern of some laity that diaconal ministers were somehow making their ministry less important. The 1992 speech in favor of ordained deacons by Lay Leader Doris Rudy (quoted in the previous chapter) was a response to these concerns.

Diaconal ministers were a new office in 1976. By 1992, many diaconal ministers had become leaders in their conferences and were demonstrating the gift that God was offering to the church through their called and set-apart ministry. Diaconal ministers were considered laity and counted in the quota system for boards and conferences that way; but with their theological training and specialized skills in ministry, they were often asked to lead conference committees. Some diaconal ministers were elected as lay delegates to the General Conferences. To many laity, diaconal ministers seemed to be clergy.

As the Council of Bishops began their discussion of the diaconate in 1992, diaconal ministers were convinced that it would be a set-back. The bishops tended to support the status quo; all of them had, of course, been ordained as deacons before their final ordination as elders. Thus, efforts to convince the church of the wisdom of an ordained diaconate in this quadrennium fell primarily to diaconal ministers, their allies, and the General Board of Higher Education and Ministry staff and its elected board of directors. They were determined to succeed.

Staff Changes at GBHEM

Roger Ireson became general secretary in 1988. He had been dealing with the tension between the two ministry divisions ever since he arrived. They did work together on the Africa University project, but opposition to the goals of the Division of Diaconal Ministry remained strong. Rosalie Bentzinger was ready to retire in 1994. She had served since 1979 and had brought diaconal ministry into the consciousness of the denomination with the help of Joaquin Garcia and Paul Van Buren. Clear standards and processes were established that insured the high quality of diaconal ministers. Still, the Division of Ordained Ministry and the Division of Diaconal Ministry were not on the same page.

In 1994, Rosalie did retire, and a search committee began to look for a replacement. Diaconal ministers Linda Marshall and Corinne Van Buren were on that committee. Their choice for the position was Jimmy Carr, a diaconal minister from the Mississippi Conference who had served on

GBHEM. He had been part of many discussions, and both
all and Van Buren believed that he would be the "best advocate to
lead into the future." General Secretary Ireson encouraged the committee
to find someone with a PhD in theology who could speak with scholarly
authority to the traditionalists in the church. But Marshall and Van Buren
advocated for Carr. They argued that Jimmy Carr *lived* his theology: "We
fought hard to get Jimmy into that role. We just felt so strongly that at that
time we needed a man to talk toe-to-toe with White men who were opposing us."

Jimmy Carr became the new associate general secretary of the Division
of Diaconal Ministry. Just the year before, The Rev. John (Jack) E. Harnish
joined the staff of the Division of Ordained Ministry as associate general
secretary. These two men had argued on opposite sides of that 1992 debate,
but they forged a friendship across those differences that would be important
after the decision of 1996. Harnish was from Michigan. Carr was from Mississippi. They represented two different parts of the church and two different cultures. The potential to heal the division between the sections of the
GBHEM staff was heightened. Jack Harnish, looking back to the situation
in 1994 wrote,

> When I came to interview for the position of Associate General Secre-
> tary for the Division of Ordained Ministry, there was concern expressed
> about how I would relate to the then separate Division of Diaconal
> Ministry. Coming into that role, the tension between the two sides of
> the Kern Building [which housed GBHEM in Nashville] was palpable.
> The two staffs were hardly speaking to each other. Ordained Ministry
> was on one side of the central vestibule, and Diaconal Ministry was on
> the other and the land between was no-man's land, with Roger Ireson
> upstairs trying to bring peace to the troops down below. I have always
> said Roger deserves immense credit for managing all that. The fact that
> Jimmy arrived soon after I did gave us an opportunity to bridge the
> great divide.

General Secretary Ireson recognized that his new leaders would need to
help both divisions move in a new direction: "I was determined to bring in
someone new who had a sense of what was at stake and what was at the heart
of the discussion." Ireson believed that Harnish and Carr would seek ways
to work together for the good of the church: "Jimmy had a gift for working
across the aisle. Jack had grown up in a conservative Methodist environment

but had grown beyond that and could relate to both the evangelical and mainline stream of the church." Ireson was pleased with his new staff in 1994, and hopeful that the feuding divisions would resolve their tension as they all moved toward the decisive General Conference of 1996.

Scholarship in Support of Diaconal Ministry Continued

In the quadrennium following the near-miss of 1992, the division continued to seek out ecumenical partners who could support their work. They worked with DIAKONIA World Organization and DOTAC (Diakonia of the Americas and Caribbean) to learn from other manifestations of the diaconate and participate in ecumenical theological discussions. In 1993, Paul Van Buren wrote a paper that listed passages in the New Testament using *diakonia* or related terms. He relied on scholarly work of John Collins, in *Diakonia: Reinterpreting the Ancient Sources* (New York: Oxford University Press, 1990). Van Buren noted that Collins "strongly criticizes what he sees as too exclusive of a connection between *diakonia* and lowly service" (Van Buren 1993, 1). Instead, Van Buren notes, Collins argues that the term was often used to indicate a messenger or go-between and that the sender is God. This was especially important because the diaconal ministers were nearly all women and could too easily be trapped in patriarchal paradigms. They needed support for their self-understanding as well as to educate the church. To think of themselves as messengers between God and the world was more empowering and prophetic than the image of themselves as loving and caring servants doing social work.

In 1994, Van Buren participated in a consultation on diaconal ministry with the Evangelical Lutheran Church in America. He wrote a report for the group on the state of diaconal ministry in The United Methodist Church. At that time, 70 percent were employed in congregations and 73 percent were female. More than 80 percent had at least one graduate degree. He also described the candidacy process and noted that the first step was to contact the Conference Board of Diaconal Ministry and begin working with a mentor (unpublished paper, 1994). Van Buren doesn't say this, but perhaps a process that began with the conference board would ensure that the potential candidate could find people who would interpret diaconal ministry accurately. Many clergy and laity were still quite uninformed.

Standards and Rituals for Diaconal Ministry

Joaquin Garcia, as director of Conference Relations for the Division of Diaconal Ministry, was coordinating the development of a handbook that would guide the Conference Boards of Diaconal Ministry when they met with candidates. Garcia also was training officers of conference boards. *Handbook for Conference Board of Diaconal Ministry*, published by the Division of Diaconal Ministry (1992) demonstrates how far the diaconal ministry had come. It recommended that each Conference Board of Diaconal Ministry be composed of one-third laity, one-third diaconal ministers, and one-third ordained elders. If there were deaconesses in the conference, they should be represented on the Board (86). Some of the board's major tasks were to meet with candidates for diaconal ministry, to verify that the candidate had met academic requirements, and to discern whether the candidate was indeed called and suited for consecration to this office. A psychological assessment had become the norm. Requirements were similarly rigorous for both diaconal ministers and elders.

Kay Barckley, a diaconal minister from the Pacific Northwest Conference, was elected to the Division of Diaconal Ministry of GBHEM and chaired the Standards Committee. Barckley recalled how they struggled, particularly with educational standards, and finally affirmed that these should be different from those required for elders. Both diaconal ministers and elders were required to complete a Bachelor's degree from an accredited institution. The candidate for diaconal ministry could qualify with a Master's degree and the Basic Graduate Theological Studies courses.[1] The Master's degree should be in a specialized field related to the ministry in which the diaconal minister would be engaged. Elders were required to have a Master of Divinity degree. Candidates who were entering diaconal ministry as a second career had other options that honored their experience. These standards supported the broadening vision of an office for ministry connecting church and world. The interview process with the Board of Diaconal Ministry was careful and mirrored the processes used by the Conference Board of Ordained Ministry.

The *Handbook* suggested joint meetings of the Conference Boards of Diaconal Ministry and Ordained Ministry (1992, 87). Funds from the Ministerial Education Fund were to be made available for both diaconal ministers and ordained clergy for continuing education or basic theological education courses (87). Boards at the conference level were being encouraged to work together.

The *Handbook* also referred to ¶307 in the 1992 *Book of Discipline*, which stated, "The Service for Consecration and the Service for Ordination may be incorporated into one service."

Combining these rituals could emphasize the similarity of the commitment of both church and individual to these ministries. The regularization and integration of diaconal ministry alongside ordained elders in each conference was establishing their similarities and their *set-apart* status. All who attended such a service could be excused if they found it difficult to distinguish between diaconal ministers and elders. Neither appeared to be laity, although diaconal ministers were still technically laity. The definition of processes and qualifications for entrance into diaconal ministry was part of the work to help The United Methodist Church see the value of a diaconal ordained office. Kay Barckley says the board was "constantly trying to make incremental steps or take the steps that we could take. We kept our eye on the vision."

Grassroots Advocacy

A small group of diaconal ministers in Tennessee led by Nan Zoller were quite frustrated with the paralysis of the 1992 General Conference. Zoller had been a delegate to Jurisdictional Conference in 1988, where she had seen there how little was known about diaconal ministry. She recalls:

> Anybody who was running for bishop would come in to meet the delegation. One person came in and we asked how he saw the diaconal minister. The answer we got was, "Well, I know one. . . ." I was just seeing that they were totally uninformed or oblivious. They were threatened, but they were uninformed.

Zoller also observed that, each time a ministry study report came out, it advocated for a permanent diaconate. The conversation would be lively, driven by both theological and missional concerns. But as the memories of General Conference faded, the conversation would dwindle. Diaconal ministers were frustrated at the lack of action and felt voiceless. With this insight and the failure in 1992, Zoller and a few others decided to start a newsletter "to keep the conversation going." They developed a list of diaconal ministers, General Conference delegates, bishops, Christian educators, and other influencers and began mailing a newsletter called "Colleagues in Dialogue." She says, "We saw that the elders we knew were either uninformed or threatened by these diaconals, who [they thought] wanted to take their place or push them out."

The newsletter went out at least twice each year of that quadrennium. It was supported by small donations from diaconal ministers and by a local group who would come together to "lick and stick" the 11x14 single sheet into envelopes for mailing. Susan Padgett was one of those volunteers. She says, "Without Nan's advocacy, we would not have had the 1996 General Conference decision that we did. She worked tirelessly for over three years to draw in people from across our denomination: lay, diaconal ministers, local pastors, and elders." The mailing list kept getting larger. Thanks to "Colleagues in Dialogue," the conversation included diverse voices and remained robust through the quadrennium. Zoller "was a pretty shrewd politician, very strategic," says Padgett. All of this work was funded by contributions and done behind the scenes by volunteers. None of them were delegates to the General Conference of 1996.

Twenty-four years had passed since the 1968 step was taken toward a permanent, ordained deacon. The affirmation of professional certification for certain ministry careers and a consecrated lay worker had blossomed and grown into diaconal ministry with high standards and processes parallel to those of the elder. Nearly every quadrennium, the General Conference had heard a proposal for a permanent ordained diaconate. However, the denomination was hanging on tightly to the tradition of ordaining eventual elders to what was essentially a transitional office, the deacon. The confusion of having transitional deacons—deacons whose goal was to become ordained elders after a probational period as deacons—and a new permanent deacon was just too much. The stalemate remained as the 1992 General Conference adjourned.

Peace Caravan to Sarajevo

Part of Joaquin Garcia's work was to continue to find ways to expand the church's understanding of diaconal ministry and to help expand the vision of diaconal ministers. One aspect of these goals was reflected in the Peace Mission Caravan initiative. The first of these sent a group of diaconal ministers to Sarajevo in 1995, shortly after a ceasefire. The goal was to experience a creative dislocation that would help participants experience God at work in a different way. Joaquin likened it to Jacob wrestling with the angel and asking for a special blessing. Like Jacob, the participants in these caravans would meet God in the experience but would be marked—changed—as Jacob was. These caravans were based on the Wesleyan concept of social holiness, which is at the root of Methodism and diaconal ministry. The group stayed in a school and repaired bullet and mortar holes in its walls. They also met many different people in attempts to understand the effects of war and to spread hopes for peace.

Following their time in Sarajevo, the members of the caravan traveled to the World Diakonia Gathering in Friedrichroda, Germany, and presented a resolution to the assembly to support the treaty to eliminate landmines. It was in this assembly that the diaconal ministers became a significant part of the worldwide Diakonia Movement. They joined in solidarity with the other members of Diakonia to urge the elimination of injustice and to work for peace; they were connecting the needs of the world to the church. This was the first of several caravans that GBHEM would organize in the years to come.

The Council of Bishops

The task of addressing the stalemate over ordaining deacons was assigned to the Council of Bishops. In 1988, William B. Oden was elected to the episcopacy from Oklahoma. He had been a delegate to General Conference several times and part of the discussions about ministry. When the 1992 General Conference voted to refer the discussion about diaconal ministry to the Council of Bishops, Oden was asked to chair the committee. He also drafted the response for the Council of Bishops in 1992–1996.

During that work, Oden asked for a copy of Rena Yocom's doctoral project, which he had heard about from Dale Dunlap. Oden sent Yocom a personal note of how helpful it was for him. Her work, *In Diakonia*, as mentioned above, employed Scripture, tradition, experience, and reason as guidelines for an investigation of the diaconate, both historically and in contemporary Christianity. Ultimately, she argued for two ordained orders: an order of elder and a permanent ordained diaconate to "hold equally the sacramental and service ministries of the church" (1991, 98). Although Yocom was pleased that her writing was helpful to the bishops, she was disappointed that the bishops' report to the 1996 General Conference recommended that diaconal ministry continue to be a lay office.

The Council of Bishops had listened to the concern expressed by several General Conferences. Instead of presenting a proposal for a change to a segment of ministry, they urged consideration of the "comprehensive whole. All the legislative recommendations are interrelated and mutually interactive. All parts contribute to the whole and must be studied and discussed in light of these relationships, not divided into segments for separate consideration" (1996 ADCA, 969). They also agreed on a compelling guiding theme for their work: "The Ministry of All Christians Expressed Through God's Mission to the World Through the Church" (969). They reported that all their decisions were made through consensus after worship, study, and listening. Then each episcopal area around the world was asked to respond to a preliminary report. "Continual rewriting grew out of each phase of the study/listening process," the report claimed (*ADCA* 1996, 970). They asked the General Conference to receive the report and to keep focused on "the Ministry of All Christians" as decisions were made.

Part I of the report was theological. It affirmed that "God continues to form a new creation through acts of courage and love that renew hope in local communities." Another interesting sentence is, "New opportunities for service, new fields of mission, new forms of devotional life, and new commitments to prayer and study challenge our complacency with familiar patterns of leadership" (971). Each of these sentences might appear to support the need for a permanent ordained deacon with gifts for these "acts of courage and love that renew hope" and that would "challenge our complacency with familiar patterns of leadership." The report defined ministry as worshiping, proclaiming, teaching, healing, serving, liberating, and reconciling (971–972). The next section of the report was subtitled, "The Apostolic Witness" (972). In this historical section, the report fails to mention the strong role of deacons in the first centuries of the church. It also affirms the importance of "ties to other communions," which might be a reference to the communions that continued to practice a sequential ordination for their priests/presbyters.

After a section on the many ways that the Methodist movement had organized itself over the centuries and the importance of lay leadership, the report includes these fascinating sentences: "Functions and titles sometimes overlap where different histories have converged on similar tasks in ministry. Changing understandings of effective organization produce new offices and roles, and the successive changes leave their traces in the pages of our *Discipline*" (974). The report also claims that, "[m]ore than most Christian traditions, ours has sought to order ministry in response to the needs of the people, rather than according to a normative pattern" (975). This last was particularly a justification for the laypersons who were used in congregations where an elder was not available. These lay pastors were authorized to preach, teach, and provide the sacraments. This practice was always a concern for ecumenical partners.

The core of the report focused on three offices: lay ministry steward, deacon, and elder. The lay ministry steward was a new proposal, designed to "provide nurture and guidance in the Christian life and to work along with ordained ministers to enable the local congregation to respond faithfully in ministry. Lay Ministry Stewards are key participants in the ministry of the local congregation, elected annually at the Charge Conference" (976). The bishops explained that a congregation could have more than one person elected to this new office; persons with mature faith and leadership potential might be recommended to the charge conference for the office. This has never been approved by a General Conference, perhaps because it seems to create a hierarchy among lay leadership or could become a sort of "pastor's pet" position.

Then the report turned to the ordained ministry:

> God calls some persons to lifetime service to the ministry of the whole church. These persons set apart with prayer and the laying on of hands (Acts 6:6) form the ordained ministry within the ministry of all Christians. Ordination is a public sign and act in which the church affirms God's gifts given for our use through the work of those who are called as ordained ministers. (976)

If you remove the next to the last word, *ordained*, these sentences describe both elders and diaconal ministers. And Acts 6 is the story of the early followers of Jesus organizing themselves so that some are set apart for study of the Word and prayer, and others for the justice work of feeding hungry people in the community. The next paragraph clarifies that "[s]ervant leadership is foundational to all ordained ministry" and "must be fully present in the ministry of the elder" (976). Nothing in this preliminary section would prevent a distinctive, permanent diaconate.

The section on deacons in the bishops' report recommended continuing the multiple types of deacons. One type of deacon would be the persons entering into probationary membership status and intending to become elders, the transitional deacon. Another would be associate members who have qualified through the local pastor and Course of Study route. The third would be a new office that would replace diaconal ministry with a permanent deacon. The bishops had acquiesced to "leaving traces of successive changes in the pages of our *Discipline*." The report stated,

> Servant leadership is foundational to all ordained ministry. Servant leadership has historically characterized the ministry of the deacon, and it must be fully present in the ministry of the elder, including the ministry of those elders charged with responsibility as superintendents. (976)

The bishops did not discontinue the transitional deacon ordination for elders. This was where the diaconal ministers would disagree with the report.

The first paragraph of the section on the ministry of the deacon contains these sentences: "In the world, the deacon seeks to express a ministry of compassion and justice, assisting laypersons as they claim their own ministry. In the congregation, the ministry of the deacon is to teach and to form disciples, and to lead worship together with other ordained and laypersons" (977). A paragraph in the middle of this section sought to justify continuing the transitional ordination practice:

> All ordained ministry requires this servant leadership of the deacon. The long practice in some of our traditions of first ordaining elders as deacons reflects this awareness. What has not been so well understood is that the ministry of the deacon has an integrity of its own. The elder must also be a deacon, but the deacon need not be an elder. Along with other Methodist bodies and other communions in the ecumenical Christian family, we see the need in our time for a permanent vocation for the deacon, and a place for persons with this vocation in the ordained ministry of the church. (977)

The section recommended that deacons be eligible to be full members of the annual conference, non-itinerant, under appointment by the bishop, and maintain a connection to a congregation even if their appointment was to a non-church or non-local-church setting. In a later section, the report recommended that the practice of consecrating diaconal ministers end. This proposal from the bishops was carefully crafted and would have moved the church much closer to the permanent ordained deacon that some believed would embody an aspect of the mission that needed more emphasis.

The pace of events began to pick up. The GBHEM board met October 5–8, 1995, and received a report of the Ministry Study Commission from the Council of Bishops. Bishop William Oden attended to make the report. The Southeast Jurisdiction Boards of Diaconal Ministry were meeting for training and received a summary of the Ministry Study report on October 9–10, 1995. In late October, a Convocation of Diaconal Ministers was held in Atlanta. The Council of Bishops would meet the first week of November, immediately following the convocation to take a final vote on the proposal that they would send to General Conference. Barbara Garcia, chair of the Board of Diaconal Ministry for the Tennessee Conference sent a message to her board, diaconal ministers, and candidates for diaconal ministry in which she urged them to "engage in prayer and reflection so that all forms of ministry will be best structured and enhanced to serve all God's people." The Tennessee Conference Board took this very seriously and submitted petitions to the General Conference that would eliminate the dual ordination for elders and replace it with consecration for a probationary period prior to full ordination and conference membership for both deacons and elders.

The 1995 National Convocation of Diaconal Ministers: "Through Exploration to Celebration"

The diaconal ministers were excited as they gathered in Atlanta. It was beginning to look like their ministry would be recognized more fully with the creation of a permanent ordained deacon and the discontinuance of the office of diaconal minister. They were about to hear from Bishop William Oden about the Ministry Study. They would also have an opportunity to hear from Dr. Mary Elizabeth Moore, who had become their primary spokesperson on the theology and history of the diaconate. About five hundred diaconal ministers attended the convocation. The timing of this gathering was to prove critical to the eventual reordering of ministry at the 1996 General Conference.

Linda Hart Marshall was part of the design team. According to her, the goal of the convocation was to "deeply explore who we were as diaconal ministers so that we could better articulate why we felt it was important to be ordained as deacons. We were trying to empower us to have a better articulation of who we are and how we can contribute to the greater good."

On Thursday, October 26, 1995 as the event began, the group was welcomed by Roger Ireson. Next to speak was Mary Elizabeth Moore. Her topic was "Exploring Theological Dimensions for Diaconal Ministry." Then Bishop Oden had the floor for an hour and presented the Ministry Study report. Following a renewal of baptism service of worship and dinner, Dr. Thomas H. Groome, professor of religious education from Boston College, spoke on "Exploring a Biblical Dimension in Diaconal Ministry: Toward an Alive, Living, and Lived Faith." Many attendees recall, twenty-five years later, how Groome encouraged the group of five hundred to put their hands on their heads and say together, "I am not the Messiah. I am not the Messiah!" He was urging them to remember that God was in it too. The group considered theological and biblical issues related to diaconal ministry on that first day and, during that, they learned about the bishops' report to the General Conference. Many were deeply concerned about the proposal, which did not discontinue the transitional deacon and its attendant hierarchical implications.

Following the evening session, Jimmy Carr, associate general secretary for the Division of Diaconal Ministry, invited everyone who wanted to talk more about the Ministry Study report to gather. Many came. Mary Elizabeth Moore remembers:

> The reaction of the diaconal ministers was huge and negative, not to the whole report, but to the two types of deacon because they recognized that if we went that way as a denomination, we would be diminishing the deacon in such a way that the vision for mission could not be lived out. I had been asked to convene the meeting. What came out of the meeting was that the deacons did not want to be silent. They wanted to speak out in a way that could be considered and heard at the next GC. And because this was already 1995 and the next GC was less than a year away and legislation would have to go in right away, the group decided that we would act. The GBHEM board staff would appoint a small team to give leadership to that work on behalf of the diaconal ministers. A team was appointed, and I was appointed chair. That happened on the spot. Jimmy did it.

The convocation participants, agitated and anxious from their action of the night before, spent half of Friday dispersed into the city and engaged in service projects. One woman still recalls that she and her friends picked up trash in a neighborhood. Diane Wasson Eberhart organized that portion of the program, which was a massive undertaking that embodied diaconal service. The diaconal ministers were energized.

The final day of the convocation celebrated the calling to service of diaconal ministers. The Rev. Minerva Carcaño spoke. Diaconal Minister N. Lynne Westfield preached, "Remember Jesus." A deeply meaningful hand-washing ritual, with bowls of water at every table, was led by diaconal ministers Joaquin and Barbara Garcia, Paul and Corinne Van Buren, and Jimmy and Joy Carr, all leaders in the denomination. As each diaconal minister's hands were washed, they were blessed for the ministry to come by those at their table. The closing worship liturgy encouraged them: "Be with us and energize us to face the challenge and the glory, the task and the reward, [o]f being in service to you, O God. Amen and Amen!" When the diaconal ministers left the gathering, many were determined to talk with General Conference delegates in their conference and to advocate for deacons ordained to Word and service who would serve as equal partners with elders. "A lot was riding on it," Linda Marshall recalls.

The Diaconal Clearness Committee

Mary Elizabeth Moore and her small group began to work together on a response to the bishops' Ministry Study report. They met during the convocation and continued to meet for the next months via conference call and email. The group included diaconal ministers from each US jurisdiction. Anita Wood was part of the committee; she remembers, "Besides preparing a response to the bishops' proposal we had to develop links in our annual conference to support it. The board staff had to stay out of it, they had been directed not to be involved." Moore was leading and described their process:

> We set it up right away as a clearness committee. We began our meetings with prayer and time for silence. In our meetings when we got to a stuck place where we were trying to figure out the best way, we would just pause and be silent. Sometimes for a few minutes. And as someone became ready to speak, we would open it back up and go back to the question at hand. That was remarkable and it helped us to remain centered and focused on God and God's leadership. It also helped us to hear each other well.

Linda Marshall calls it a "phenomenal experience."

Moore guided the group with a sure hand: "We decided very early in our process that the bishop's proposal was actually very well done. We saw ourselves as improving upon it rather than contradicting it." She had learned from her previous experiences with General Conference that the legislation needed to be thorough and detailed. The conference was not equipped to deal with big ideas unless they were accompanied by all the Disciplinary changes necessary to implement them.

Moore was staying with her mother, who was recovering from surgery when she had what she calls a "come-to-Jesus moment."

> I was sitting at the table. It was 2 am. I was deeply in the weeds working on the particularities of the legislation. And I said to myself, Mary Elizabeth, you're either going to do this all the way or this isn't going to be effective. I stopped and prayed. And what came to me is, you need to give it everything you've got. And I decided that it was my calling. I worked on that legislation all night, for multiple nights. And then I would send it to the team.

One decision they made has had long-term repercussions and is not yet resolved. That is the question of sacraments. Ordination and sacraments have been linked together since the earliest years of Christianity. As Linda Marshall recalls, the Clearness Committee was "trying to clarify what were the strong talking points and what were negotiation points." Their process identified that "sacraments were one of the things that we could give on if that was going to prevent us from becoming an order." The Clearness Committee agreed, however, that the deacon needed to be distinct from the elder. If elders continued to be ordained first as deacons, it would detract from those called to the ministry of the deacon; their single ordination would look like it was partial. This was not open to negotiation.

They also strategized about how they could get a fair hearing from the General Conference. According to Moore,

> We recognized that even though we had people in the legislative committee in 1992 who were articulate and were able to make a case well, who understood the vision, understood the diaconate, understood the church structures and all the rest, and the theology of ministry, we didn't have the space for actually making that case and having it considered more seriously without making it contentiously. We realized it might be more helpful to have a layperson as chair of the legislative committee and not to have any of us who had been part of this proposal process in leadership roles. Specifically, people said to me they did

not want me in a leadership role because they wanted me to be free to speak. We had people who knew people and people who were thoughtful about what kind of strategy would create the space where we could even consider this well. So that's exactly what happened.

The Diaconal Ministry Clearness Committee submitted about thirty petitions, which were listed in the Advance Daily Christian Advocate (ADCA) as Proposed Changes to the Ministry Study (1996, 1502–1502). That heading was important; the Clearness Committee did not want to be seen as disrespectful. They wanted their proposals to be seen as supporting the work of the bishops but offering clarifications. Each petition was carefully crafted and amended the bishops' legislation, retaining as much language as possible. The Clearness Committee proposal deleted ordination as a deacon from the section on elders and replaced it with consecration as a probationary member of the annual conference. This consecration to probationary membership was for both deacons and elders.

The Tennessee Conference Board of Diaconal Ministry also submitted petitions that would eliminate sequenced ordination for elders.

By this time, the rationale to eliminate the ordination of probationary deacons had clarified. Joaquin and Barbara Garcia recall them:

1. The probationary status was not an order.
2. The original Order of Deacon as it was conceived and practiced by the early church was not a steppingstone toward the ordination of a priest.
3. The Methodist Protestant Church, one of our predecessor denominations, did not have a probationary deacon.
4. The Evangelical United Brethren, also a predecessor denomination, did not have a probational deacon.
5. In the 1970s and 1980s, the UMC became clearer about our theological understanding and our affirmation that we believe in one baptism; similarly, there is no theological rationale for dual ordination.

The members of the Clearness Committee were well prepared for General Conference when it convened in Denver in April 1996. And perhaps the time was right. Joaquin Garcia calls it "a *kairos* moment for the deacon." Rena Yocom, who had been there at the beginning and was a seasoned participant in ecumenical dialogue, also sees it as the right change for the moment. Yocom explains,

There have been times in church history when the sacramental ministry of the church in the sanctuary was not sufficient. The church needed to be seen, out in the world. At the end of the twentieth century, there was so much upheaval: a change in world powers, the fall of the Soviet Union, the many wars, homelessness, migration of peoples from country to country. This was the time when we needed this expression of the church. And the church needed to authenticate this ministry in the world.

The stage was set.

The Legislative Committee

The bishops were given time early in the General Conference agenda to make a report on the Ministry Study. It was April 18, a Thursday. The stage had been set the night before by Bishop Judith Craig, who asked the delegates "to gather together around the table, prayerfully attempting to discern God's will for our Church" (*DCA* 1996, 76). Bishop David Lawson and Bishop Sharon Brown Christopher presented a summary of the report. They began with their proposal for a lay ministry steward and described the affirmation process for the new office as "similar to persons seeking pastoral ministry."

Then they discussed a new understanding of the ordained deacon that would "express a ministry of compassion and justice" and assist laypersons to "claim their own ministry." The presenters explained that the new deacon's role in the congregation is "to teach and to inform disciples, to lead worship together with other ordained persons and laity, to celebrate the sacrament of baptism, to assist the elders in the sacrament of the Lord's Supper" (77).

The elder section contained the following statement: "We affirm the continuing responsibility of the elder to fulfill their servant leadership as deacons, while serving as elders." This document reaffirmed the sequential ordination for elders but tried to redefine *deacon* somewhat in response to the calls for more intentional ministry in the world (78).

Bishop Christopher gave instructions to the delegates. She stressed listening for the guidance of the Spirit and the ideas of colleague delegates. The delegates were sent out of the hall to assigned reflection groups. A moderator and recorder had been designated for each group. The groups were instructed to allow anyone to talk who wished to. The recorder would capture the discussion and listen for points of consensus, issues needing clarification, and concerns. These recorded notes would then be given to a group of compilers who would "prepare a written statement of what has been discerned," and it would be passed on to the legislative committee (79). As the delegates left the hall to find their reflection groups, they were singing, "Here I Am, Lord." The General Conference was challenged to attend to the Holy Spirit as they listened to one another in response.

The legislative committee with responsibility for the ministry petitions was given the summary of those discussions when it began its work the next day. This time, the diaconal ministers and their allies were well prepared for the committee process. Quite a few diaconal ministers agreed to attend the General Conference as observers in order to keep watch on the legislative committee and be ready to offer support if needed. Linda Marshall was one of those observers. This meant that she could sit in on the discussions of the legislative committee and help strategize or provide resources. As chair of the GBHEM Division of Diaconal Ministry and a member of the Clearness Committee, she brought a great deal of expertise to the room. She remembers:

> It was a whole different experience than '92. We had learned how to talk across the aisle. We leadership had learned a lot from each other. There were still some anxious moments for sure. We were careful that we were not stuck up on the podium for votes. Got our talking-point handout to all delegates at certain times. We did a lot more behind the scenes conversation than we had done before. And we found allies— Kelly Bender turned out to be one—a White, heterosexual elder who said, "I believe in the role of the deacon. I will help you get other advocates like me." Those were critical times.

When the legislative committee convened, it elected Sandra Lutz, a lay woman from East Ohio, as its chair and Earl Bledsoe as vice chair. This was what the advocates for an ordained deacon had hoped and planned for. Now Mary Elizabeth Moore and others who were prepared to support the Clearness Committee proposal were able to speak more freely in the discussion.

Sandra Lutz was an experienced delegate who had also served as a director of the General Commission on the Status and Role of Women. Lutz' strategy was to encourage people to talk it out: "We were trying to get people to change long standing beliefs. When you do that, you need to be somewhat gentle with it. To demean that or make light of their passion about that" would be counter-productive. A number of diaconal ministers had come to the General Conference, such as Linda Marshall, who had worked on petitions and had been part of the Division of Diaconal Ministry. They had resources and information that they could offer when needed. Lutz saw them at work. She says,

> Deacons are good listeners, patient folks. It affirmed what they felt called to. People like Linda and others. They were doing that role right there at General Conference. I remember the deacons always checking. If it got late at night, they would be there with cookies. Or, getting something cold to drink. All of that made it possible for others to do the job that they could do. They became part of the process. It was a real gift.

The bishops' Ministry Study report had come with hundreds of petitions to bring the *Discipline* into compliance with their proposals. The compilation of the reflection groups' responses was available to the legislative committee. The Diaconal Clearness Committee also had prepared nearly thirty petitions with their proposed amendments to the Ministry Study report. Most were aimed at eliminating the sequential ordination for elders and creating a new order of deacon. They also clarified the relationship between the ordained deacon and the congregation: "The deacon embodies the interrelationship between worship in the gathered community and service to God in the world" (*ADCA* 1996, 1503). The legislation coming from the Diaconal Clearness Committee was careful and thorough. Accompanying it was legislation from the Tennessee Conference Board of Diaconal Ministry, which also deleted the sequential ordination for elders and created a probationary period for both elders and deacons prior to ordination and full conference membership.

With so much legislation to consider, the legislative committee decided to divide into ten subgroups. Nine diaconal ministers were voting lay members of the legislative committee so they could spread out and provide representation in all the subcommittees. Barbara Garcia, chair of the Tennessee Board of Diaconal Ministry, was in the group considering petitions related to probationary membership. Also, in that group were Jack Harnish, Lovett Weems (president of Saint Paul School of Theology), and Larry Goodpaster (delegate from Mississippi who was elected bishop in 2000). They determined that using "consecration" as the liturgical act for entrance into this relationship was confusing, although several petitions had used that term; diaconal ministers, church buildings, and bishops were consecrated. But what to call it? Sometime late on Friday night, Garcia's group chose "commissioning" to designate entrance into the probationary period leading to ordination to the Order of Elder or Deacon. The term felt right for these people who were being sent out (appointed) by the bishop. A cryptic little note in the *Daily Christian Advocate* on April 22 reported:

> The committee worked Friday and Saturday to bring all legislation related to the Ministry Study in line with the decisions made Friday morning to recommend a common probationary period. The committee approved legislation that moved away from sequential ordination to a single ordination for deacons and elders. The committee also struggled to determine the title for a person in probationary membership and after considerable attempts decided on the term commissioning. Additional actions incorporate many of the suggested changes from the Diaconal Ministers Clearness Committee into Paragraphs 306 through 315. (201)

The *DCA* names the authors of this little note as Linda Green and Judy Smith. They chose words that name the actions but tell little of the very hard work that went on in that legislative committee. Their decision to create a common probationary period was pivotal and created a deacon that could stand alongside the elder and take a complementary but different role in the mission of the church.

Legislative Committee Chair Sandy Lutz was fully aware of the commitments of the Division of Diaconal Ministry of GBHEM. She had served as a lay member of the board in that division for eight years. She had learned a lot about the theological and ecclesial arguments both for and against this re-ordering of ministry. She also knew that, as chair, she would have opportunities to "let the voices be heard that I knew had the answers." Although the legislative committee had a huge workload, Lutz led them masterfully through the process, and they reached agreement with much less rancor and discord than had been present in 1992. "Nobody ever doubted that we were doing the right thing," claims Lutz.

The legislative committee voted nonconcurrence with the bishops' proposal for a lay ministry steward. It voted to delete the sequential ordination—the transitional deacon—for elders. It voted to "commission" deacons and elders when they entered probationary membership. And it voted to support a new order of ordained deacon. No minority report came from the committee. Its members had reached a strong consensus. The next step was to bring it to the plenary of the 1996 General Conference.

6 The Birth of the UMC Deacon

The 1996 General Conference and Its Aftermath

Even though the legislative committee was proposing an ordained deacon with full conference membership and discontinuing the transitional form of deacon, only General Conference action could make it reality. And even if it was passed by the General Conference plenary, many more pieces needed to fall into place. The GBHEM would have primary responsibility for enacting the new legislation; diaconal ministers would need to decide whether they were called to ordination; Boards of Ordained Ministry in each conference would need to interview and approve (or refuse to approve) candidates for ordination; bishops would need to ordain them. 1996–1997 would be the year of many transitions.

The 1996 General Conference

When it came time for the legislative committee to report to the plenary about the ministry legislation, the General Conference was abuzz—not only about this legislation, but also because a group of bishops, who came to be known as The Denver 15, had written a statement in which they urged the church to cease its condemnation of homosexuality. That statement caused quite a stir. The conference was filled with conversations and controversy. The atmosphere was electric.

Many United Methodists were pleased and relieved that some episcopal voices had spoken out in support of justice and acceptance for LGBTQ persons. Others were angry that these bishops were openly speaking out against the official stance of the church that "homosexuality is incompatible with Christian teaching" (*Discipline*, ¶304.3). Behind closed doors, the Council of Bishops berated the fifteen colleagues who had publicly exposed their lack of unanimity. This issue dominated the conversations in the hallways, and emotions were running high!

The debate about human sexuality had been going on since the 1972 General Conference. Those debates often seemed to eclipse other issues. Even exciting new missional legislation might be overshadowed by the disagreement about human sexuality and Christian values. Rena Yocom remarks that the 1976 General Conference had easily approved the diaconal ministry, perhaps because the more controversial issue that year was sexuality. Potentially, 1996 was no different.

The narrative of this book has ignored many other important actions before the General Conferences. Including those would extend the book to several volumes and overwhelming complexity. The sexuality debates, for example, have dominated every General Conference, and 1996 was no exception.

The United Methodist Church is basically a representative democracy. The delegates to each General Conference are elected about a year in advance. They then study the legislation when it is published. All the legislation must be available in several languages because this is a global church. The General Conference meets for about two weeks every four years. It takes on a different personality each time, but the proceedings are always made more complex by the use of Roberts Rules of Order. Often, one is voting on an amendment to an amendment. Keeping track of whether a yes or no will get you to the desired decision is challenging.

Only two or three people are recognized to speak on an issue in an attempt to keep the process moving. But even that is political, as the presiding bishop may call on someone they know or who has been associated with the topic at hand. The diaconal ministers advocating for a new ordained deacon had learned this the hard way in 1992; they were much more prepared to get the right voices to the microphone at the 1996 General Conference.

The General Conference is not only political, however; it is also deeply spiritual. Every day begins with worship and stops often for prayer. In the midst of acrimonious debate, the presiding bishop may stop and take time for the delegates to pray for discernment. United Methodists seek the guidance of the Holy Spirit even while they are strategizing and organizing to get their petitions approved! The important proposals for reordering ministry were going to be introduced into a complicated emotional, spiritual, and cultural setting in the middle of the second week of meetings.

The ministry-related legislative items were on the agenda for Wednesday evening, April 24, 1996. Linda Marshall, who had been in the thick of it during the debacle of 1992, knew that things had to happen differently this time around. After the consensus forged in the legislative committee, the proposals were ready for the plenary to act.

The chair of each legislative committee is usually the person who presents the committee's report to the plenary. Chairperson Sandra Lutz presented the report of the Ordained and Diaconal Ministry legislative committee to the 1996 General Conference on Wednesday, April 24, 1996. Lutz was an experienced participant in General Conference, and she brought a steady and sure presence to the microphone. Her speech began with a delightful story:

> At a meeting of the Divisions of Ordained and Diaconal Ministry earlier this quadrennium, Judy Smith told of a meeting where a panel of distinguished persons presented reports that documented, in unrelenting fashion, the terrible conditions of the world. After these reports, there was silence. Then one woman in the audience raised her hand and said, "'I understand how terrible things are. Would it help if I baked a cake?"

After the laughter died down, Lutz turned to the first chapter of the bishops' report on the ministry of all Christians. She reminded the delegates that "it is more important that our structure honor God's call on all our lives than that we hold to historic patterns which, although once effective, may now interfere with our ability to move ahead" (*DCA* 1996, 693–694). Unlike the legislative committee chair in 1992, Lutz believed in this new pattern for ordained ministry. She carefully constructed her presentation to lead them to this idea.

The committee had prepared a brief, summary document of their work, and it was in the delegates' hands as she spoke. Lutz worked through the report section by section. She told the delegates that the legislative committee affirmed the first chapter of the bishops' report on the ministry of all Christians with only minor amendments. However, they could not affirm the proposal for the new office of lay ministry steward in chapter 2. When the General Conference convened the previous week, all delegates had participated in reflection groups to discuss the Bishops' Ministry Study report. Evidently, the reflection groups had not been ready to accept the new lay ministry steward either. That proposal came to the plenary with a committee vote of nonconcurrence.

Lutz then turned to the committee's affirmation of two distinct orders of ordained ministry: the deacon and the elder. Both deacons and elders would be members of the annual conference in full connection. The elder would itinerate, and the deacon would not. Both orders would be appointed by the bishop. The committee also affirmed that both orders would require graduate theological education, and candidates should participate in a joint candidacy process. All this had been in the Bishops' Ministry Study report.

Next, Lutz revealed the crucial place where the legislative committee parted ways with the bishops. The committee had supported the petitions brought by Mary Elizabeth Moore and the Diaconal Clearness Committee that would "provide parallel paths leading to single ordination to each of the two distinct orders" (*DCA* 1996, 694). Single ordination for elders would create parity between the orders as well as distinct identities. She asked them to look at the back side of the summary document, which described the path to ordination. Here, the three-year probationary period as a commissioned deacon or elder was included as part of the journey from membership in a United Methodist congregation to ordination. Several times, Lutz used the phrase "service, Word, sacrament, and order" to describe the work of the elder. Because they would no longer be ordained as deacons, the call to service would be included explicitly in their ordination as elders. She was trying to forestall objections to the loss of *service*, which had previously been connected with ordination to the transitional deacon.

Lutz concluded her explanation with these words: "God's Spirit right now seems to be moving among us, gently nudging and encouraging us to take heart, breathing life into the dry bones, and calling us to trust new models and new understandings of ministry" (695). She had awakened in the middle of the night with the image of the dry bones coming to life. It felt to her like a powerful metaphor for the action that the delegates were about to take.

Then Lutz turned to legislation. She reported that the lay ministry steward petitions were on the nonconcurrence consent calendar and thus, no action was needed. That idea would be referred to the General Board of

Discipleship. That meant that the first calendar item requiring a vote concerned a single ordination for either order, essentially eliminating the traditional practice of sequential ordination for elders. This was the ultimate test for the new ordained deacon. The outcome of this vote would reveal whether the General Conference was going to make the change and recognize the distinctive role for the deacon. The legislative committee had voted concurrence, 92 to 12.

Rev. Larry Goodpaster came to the microphone to present this piece of legislation. Goodpaster was a shrewd choice to present this section because he was then an elder from the Southeast Jurisdiction, an area of the church that tended to be traditional. Jimmy Carr, who was heading the Division of Diaconal Ministry at GBHEM, was also from Mississippi. No doubt, these two colleagues had discussed this many times in the years leading up to this moment. Goodpaster's argument included a definition of *ordination* as "an act of the church which acknowledges God's call according to the talents, gifts, and abilities the person has received." He continued, "The act of ordination sets persons apart for various ministries. One of our questions is, 'Why is it necessary to set persons apart twice?'" (696).

Predictably, J. Lawrence McCleskey, a clergy delegate from Western North Carolina, was the first to be recognized by presiding Bishop Melvin Talbert, and McCleskey raised the same objection that he had in 1992: "If we adopt the proposal of the committee, we will depart from almost 1,700 years of tradition which has characterized most of Christendom" (696). He also claimed that, ever since Francis Asbury, American Methodists had done it that way and so do some of our ecumenical connections, especially Roman Catholics. Bishop Talbert then called on Mary Elizabeth Moore, who was seated with her delegation this time and not disenfranchised by sitting on the stage. She was ready to counter his argument. "I think the question before us tonight is the question of where we are going, and where is God calling us into this future?" She drew on the metaphor of *journey* to describe the developing understanding of the ministry of all Christians as servant ministry: "The base of our ministry is in baptism not in the diaconate." She continued,

> We've had study team after study team. They have done magnificent work. Almost every time they have brought the recommendation of two distinct ordinations: one to deacon, one to elder. Last time, that particular recommendation came out of legislative committee and was defeated on the floor of this General Conference by two votes. . . . If

the ministry of the Christian church is grounded in baptism, then the servanthood of all Christians is the ground from which all ministry comes. We don't therefore need to be ordained first as deacons. And we might ask ourselves, where is God calling us into the future? What vessels do we need as we journey beyond the edge of the map? (697)

Moore finally had a good opportunity to speak directly to McCleskey's appeal to tradition. After two more speeches for and two more against, the work of the legislative committee and the amendments from the Diaconal Clearness Committee were put to the test. The vote was on McCleskey's amendment that would have rejected their proposal for a probationary period beginning with commissioning, and instead, return to the proposal from the bishops for continuing the sequential ordination of those seeking to be elders. The vote was 224 yes and 710 no. McCleskey's amendment was soundly defeated. The supporters of the new deacon must have heaved a big sigh of relief! The 1996 General Conference was going to support them.

Following that groundbreaking vote, various questions were raised and answered. The committee was prepared, and the responses were gracious as well as authoritative. A delegate asked for definitions of *consecrate, commission,* and *ordain.* Mary Elizabeth Moore spoke:

> The words *consecration* and *ordination* have been used interchangeably throughout Christian history. They basically mean, "to be set apart for holy service." The word *commissioning* has to do with sending out together in mission. Co-missioning. And the word *commissioning* has been used in our tradition in terms of commissioning people for short term service, and also commissioning people to lifetime service, such as we commission missionaries and deaconesses; we commission class leaders; and we commission groups who are going out on a work team. The choice of the legislative committee was a choice for sending people out in mission together with the idea that we might envision the probationary period in a way that we've never been able to envision it before. (700)

Other small amendments to wording were proposed. None of them were substantive, and the committee quickly and graciously accepted them. Eventually, a delegate moved to suspend the rules and call the question. The body was ready to vote. They suspended the rules and then approved the document by 769 votes, an overwhelming majority!

Immediately after that vote, Sandra Lutz came back to the platform. Her first words were, "I'm sorry to be running. We don't have enough pads up here, and I wanted to vote on that particular thing." She was subtly reminding the body that proponents of this legislation had been effectively disenfranchised in 1992 because there were no voting pads on the platform, and they had been told they did not need to have a reserve in their place. Bishop Talbert must have been well aware of this history. He responded, "Let me just check this out. I think it's important for you committee members not to be disenfranchised." Then the bishop suggested that members of the committee should wait to come forward until they were ready to speak. Lutz responded, "Thank you for that advice. We thought there would be enough pads up here" (701). The subtext to this exchange must have been apparent to many in the house!

The plenary had completed their work on only one of twelve items from the legislative committee that were on that day's agenda. The next was the section on the Ministry of All Christians, which would become ¶110. It passed with 867 yes votes. And then they worked their way through several more petitions. In each case, questions were raised, and amendments were offered, but the work of the bishops along with the revisions from the Diaconal Clearness Committee were strongly upheld. The new order of ordained deacon became a reality. Diaconal ministers were laity; the new deacon would be ordained clergy with full membership in the annual conference. Elders would no longer be deacons. These actions marked the significant shift from 1976 to 1996.

The Aftermath

On the night of April 24, 1996, when the session ended, Jimmy Carr called Rosalie Bentzinger right away to tell her the news. The ordained deacon, which she believed in so fervently and had fought for so long, had finally come to pass. She was so pleased! And Jimmy Carr did not forget her contribution. They celebrated together over the telephone.

Mary Elizabeth Moore had given so much to the effort; I asked her what it was like to be there when it happened. She recalls:

The minute this decision was made, there was loud applause, but somewhat muted in contrast to the response to accepting the new hymnal that happened earlier at the same General Conference, even though it was a decision that was an overwhelming majority. But my delegation gathered around me spontaneously. They thanked me for my leadership; they recognized how much I had given to it, and they prayed for me. I have no idea how many of them voted positively or negatively. But that didn't matter. They recognized that I was part of their family and they wanted to pause with me in prayer. At the same time our bishop sent word to me that he wanted to speak with me, and he came over and sought me out. He said, "Mary Elizabeth, I know what you have given to this and I just want you to know that I appreciate all your work and I am thinking about you, holding you close in prayer because this is a momentous decision for the church and you have given yourself to it fully." Now I don't know if he supported it. But he was giving me support which I greatly appreciated.

Others were not so generous. Moore said that some people began to turn away when they met her in the hotel or corridor. And she is still grieving an encounter with a bishop who said, "You know we blame you for this whole thing, this whole debacle about the diaconate." She has endured this kind of ostracizing since 1996. Some people have not embraced the move away from tradition that was made by this General Conference. But Moore also experienced reconciliation four years later when she was invited to be the deacon at the Eucharistic table for the opening worship celebration of a denominational event. Bishop Oden was the presider. In leading that service, Moore felt a gracious acceptance by Oden and, by extension, by all the bishops. It was a healing moment. "The church is bigger than its controversies," she said.

Several diaconal ministers were lay delegates to the 1996 General Conference. Each of them remembers that momentum was behind the new ordained deacon. Diane Wasson Eberhart, an Iowa Conference diaconal minister remembers "being kind of on the edge of my seat wondering if it was going to go through. And wow! It passed! It felt miraculous. Nothing could stop it. It was going to happen." Don Ehlers, then a diaconal minister from Missouri, recalls, "It wasn't bucking the current. It just felt like it was going to happen." According to David Dodge, diaconal minister delegate from Florida, there "was a sense that the tide had turned." Looking back from nearly twenty-five years, Linda Hart Marshall says, "I believe the grace of God helped us turn our anger into movement, and we started to operate with grace." After so many years of resistance to anything that would back away from the tradition of sequential ordination, the 1996 General Conference was converted.

Jack Harnish remembers that he and Jimmy Carr were sitting together in the observer seats when the legislative committee report was considered. As the votes were taken, they looked at each other and realized that it was going to be up to them to help the conferences make this change. According to Harnish, "The honest truth is that, after the 1996 General Conference ended, we had to be ready to train conference boards in the fall. It was just amazing that we were able to pull that off." The first task was to merge the Division of Ordained Ministry and the Division of Diaconal Ministry, the same divisions that had been deeply divided for many years. Harnish credits the good relationship between himself and Carr for their success in this merger. "I've always believed that if Jimmy and I hadn't been able to work together, our staffs would be at each other's throats and the church would fumble its way forward without leadership." Harnish gives Jimmy Carr the credit because he was "smart and warm, disciplined and smooth" and he "knew how to get things done."

Harnish also credits Roger Ireson with being willing to have strong people around him who worked together to put new procedures in place to implement the General Conference actions. Overnight, two separate boards in every annual conference needed to become one. They had to clarify how this new board would process and evaluate candidates. Most of the forms and handbooks had to be rewritten and reprinted. The diaconal ministers who wanted to transition to ordination deserved a fair hearing and appropriate recognition of this big step. The ordinal had to be revised; Moore met with that committee to consult about the language for the ordination of the new deacons. So much had to happen. And it did. Every annual conference with diaconal ministers who sought ordination was able to mount an appropriate service by the next summer.

Formation Events for Diaconal Ministers Considering Ordination

Once the handbooks were ready and the Boards of Ordained Ministry were trained, the diaconal ministers who were discerning if they were called to ordination needed attention. Formation events were offered in each jurisdiction early in 1997. All diaconal ministers were encouraged—basically required—to attend one of these. They were opportunities to consider what it would mean to be ordained, to clarify one's call and identity, and to learn more about the vision for the deacon. A group gathered to help plan these transition events. Convocations would be offered in six areas of the United States. Joaquin Garcia asked Linda Hart Marshall to help plan them. Marshall recalls bringing about eight people together with expertise in such events. Dr. Linda Vogel was one of those and really helped the planning process to move quickly. "I just sat back in awe of how her mind worked," Marshall commented.

Evidently, the plans were well conceived. Twenty-five years later, many of those who attended still have powerful memories. One woman wrote, "The call [to ordination] was clear, which I certainly did not expect. That event changed my life. The time of silence, the foot washing, the support of many others from the area. I was hearing my call so *loudly* that it was overwhelming." Another participant, Rick Buckingham, was particularly moved by the "presentations of the deacons brought in from the Episcopal Church and the Uniting Church of Australia. The sense that we as United Methodists were part of an international movement toward the restoration of an ancient order of word and service with New Testament roots was very powerful." He too received "a powerful reassurance" that he had heard a call to ordination.

Interviews with the Board of Ordained Ministry

At about the same time, diaconal ministers who discerned a call to ordination were preparing their papers for an interview with the Conference Board of Ordained Ministry. The *Book of Discipline* (1996) section on requirements states in ¶321.3, that, after serving under appointment as a probationary member, a candidate should undergo "a written or oral doctrinal examination administered by the board of ordained ministry. The candidate shall demonstrate the ability to communicate clearly in both oral and written form." It also declares that the candidate "shall be able to articulate the call of God to the order of deacon . . . and to relate that call to leadership within the ministry of all Christians." In the North Georgia Conference, where I was serving at the time, we had to write answers to all the questions and then be interviewed by the Board of Ordained Ministry. In retrospect, the elders on the interview teams who had not been part of all the debates leading up to the new order must have been mystified. Some diaconal ministers were disappointed that the questions they were asked seemed inappropriate or irrelevant, but, in their defense, the elders had a lot to learn. Diaconal ministers who were in good standing had the option of applying for ordination. Thirty-seven of us were ordained in the North Georgia Conference in June 1997 under the transitional provisions for diaconal ministers in good standing (*Journal of the North Georgia Conference 1997*, 248).

In addition, the new legislation called for the formation of an "order" for each ordained office—an order for elders and an order for deacons. That new section of the *Discipline* was particularly well conceived. The Disciplinary paragraphs had been perfected and approved by the General Conference. But the whole idea of *orders* was new, especially for elders. In many conferences, the order of deacon quickly pulled together. The former diaconal ministers had known one another and advocated for ordination; they were already a community. In many conferences, the notion of elders coming together to form an order was more difficult to grasp.

The creation of orders for deacons and elders is an aspect of the 1996 legislation that has never been fully realized in many annual conferences, although it is still in the *Discipline*. The 1996 *Discipline* defined an *order* as "a covenant community within the church to mutually support, care for, and hold accountable its members" (¶311). Bishops convened the orders and then the orders elected a chairperson. The new section III of the chapter on ordained ministry ended with, "Acceptance of the status of full membership will constitute a commitment to regular participation in the life of the Order" (¶314). Elders suddenly found that they had another obligation as they lost their explicit identity as deacons. For a few elders, it felt like something had been taken away and an unwanted meeting added. No wonder some were anxious and resisting!

In early summer of 1997, many diaconal ministers were ordained as deacons. My experience was that the bishop and the worship committee of the annual conference were making up rules for how to do it right down to the last few minutes. A ruling on who could accompany each ordinand to the stage and who could lay hands on her or him was up in the air. Finally, the bishop allowed a spouse or important family member to accompany each of us, just as was the practice with elders. In some ways, this is like Mary Elizabeth Moore's description of her consecration as a diaconal minister in 1977, when it was brand new. She recalled that the decision for diaconal ministry rather than ordained ministry had been intense for her. As the service began, she was fully aware of her seminary classmates who would be ordained deacons that night. Their families were present; the ordinands were all wearing new robes. Celebrations were planned. The earlier candidates for consecration wore borrowed robes or cast-off choir robes. Moore recalls:

> We were a motley looking crew. We walked in at the end of the line. We had one or two people who were saying, "I'm not sure exactly what this means but it's going to be interesting." The people who were being ordained as deacon and elder were entering into something that the church understood. They had prepared and celebrated it well. That was not true for the rest of us. I sat in that service with tears falling down my face for parts of the service. I never even in that moment questioned the decision I had made. I only recognized that I was entering into a pathway that was filled with an unsettled relationship with the church even for some who were entering into the pathway at the same time I was.

Likewise, after the decision of 1996, the newly ordained deacons were finding their way into the new relationship. Now they voted with elders in the clergy session. Deacons now were rightfully addressed by the title *reverend*. But their pathway was definitely in an "unsettled relationship with the church."

One of the confusions related to the decision that sacramental presidency would be limited to elders. Deacons could stand at the altar, but they could not consecrate the elements. This created a feeling that deacons are second class. One well-meaning layperson, after I had preached one Sunday, said to me, "That sermon was wonderful. When are you going to be a real minister?" Those little moments do add up. The debate about sacraments and their relationship to ordination continues.

Nevertheless, an Amazing New Order of Ministry

God used our messy legislative process, and the Holy Spirit helped to move us into a creative new order of ministry by changing minds and hearts. When one compares the new order of deacon as created by the 1996 General Conference of The United Methodist Church to deacons in other communions, this one is more closely aligned with the mission of the church and more clearly equal to the elder/presbyter.

Two differences are critical. Because the transitional deacon for elders was discontinued, the United Methodist deacon is a distinctive call and a distinctive order. And because United Methodist deacons are educated alongside the elders, their graduate education is parallel. Other deacons, such as Roman Catholics, are educated in diocesan schools. Some, such as those in the Episcopal Church, serve alongside transitional deacons, which makes them look temporary or incomplete. Sacramental authority varies. Roman Catholic deacons may offer five of the seven sacraments but may not officiate at the mass. UMC deacons may only assist elders who preside, unless they have special permission from the bishop. The United Methodist deacon is complementary to the elder, rather than competing. It is intended to be a full-time, lifelong identity. The United Methodist deacon stands alone in its strong, distinctive place in the denomination. The explicit mission of The United Methodist Church—"to make disciples of Jesus Christ for the transformation of the world"—calls for two distinct orders of ordained ministry, one focused on the disciples and one focused on the church's mission in the world. Given the long years of study, reports, debate, and resistance that led up to this decision, it is quite amazing that it turned out so strong.

Looking back to 1996 as a watershed moment makes sense, but it was really the culmination of many years of discussion and evolving theological understandings of both ministry and ecclesiology. In 1964, the General Conference of the Methodist Church received a petition from the committee to study the ministry which had been meeting through the quadrennium 1960–1964. The *DCA* for May 6, 1964 reported: "The Committee on the Ministry recommends that the General Conference receives with appreciation the Report of the Study of the Ministry 1960–64 and acceptance of its recommendations, with the exception of the recommendation for a single ordination and an office of deacon." There it was—a similar proposal! The church had considered these ideas for at least thirty years before accepting them. From professional certifications in the predecessor denominations, to a consecrated lay worker in 1968, to the diaconal minister in 1976, to the birth of the ordained deacon in 1996 was a journey into fuller expression of God's call to build the kin-dom. The World Council of Churches and the Second Vatican Council cast a vision that The United Methodist Church responded to repeatedly. All Christians are called to ministry; deacons are particularly focused on leading laity from the church into the world in pursuit of God's will for compassion and justice.

7 Perfecting, Consolidating, and Strengthening the Understanding of the Deacon

1997 and After

When all the 1997 annual conferences had ended and many diaconal ministers had been ordained, the new deacons went to their appointments. Most returned to lead the same ministries they had before ordination. In some conferences, the district superintendents forgot that deacons should be on the appointment lists. So many forms needed to be corrected, and so many church groups now needed to include a representative from the new order of deacon! Some of the bishops and district superintendents who had been ordained as transitional deacons years before complained about the added burden of work.

Nearly all district superintendents needed to learn about secondary appointments (with a congregation), which were required for deacons whose primary appointment was not in a congregation. The secondary appointment was a concrete, explicit link for the deacon to a congregation. As they participated in the congregation, deacons would bring the needs of the world to the congregation. The intention was that the deacon would assist the elder with worship. Deacons are ordained to Word, service, compassion, and justice. One way to express the ordination to Word would be through liturgical functions. Of course, deacons would also be teaching, interpreting the Scriptures, and contributing to the formation of United Methodists. The secondary appointment was never intended to be a second job but to formalize the linkage between the deacon's ministry and the church. The deacon's presence at the eucharistic table would symbolize that linkage. Both deacons and elders were learning about this new relationship.

Some bishops recognized the leadership potential of these new deacons, appointing them to some positions that had been formerly held by elders. For instance, Bishop Kenneth L. Carder invited Barbara Garcia, then a diaconal minister in the Tennessee Conference to join his staff as administrative assistant in 1996. By the time she began this work in midsummer, she was enroute to ordination as a deacon. Garcia was the first deacon to serve as assistant to the bishop in The United Methodist Church. She held this position under three different bishops—Carder, William W. Morris, and Richard J. Wills Jr.—and retired in 2007. Several deacons have served as assistant to the bishop in other conferences since then. This is a position of great responsibility, which requires a person of tact, grace, and trustworthiness. Since 1997, deacons have chaired Boards of Ordained Ministry in several conferences. Deacons have been elected as clergy delegates to General and Jurisdictional Conferences. Deacons serve in conference staff positions and on General agency staff. Deacons are even leading their delegations to General Conference. Deacons have been important participants in the discussions about the future of the denomination. Deacons are recognized as influential clergy who are essential leaders for the denomination, reminding us of our mission to transform the world.

General Conference Actions

Every General Conference since 1996 has received petitions that relate to the deacon. At the General Conferences in Pittsburgh (2004), Ft. Worth (2008), and Tampa (2012), some petitions tried to lessen or undo the 1996 decision. That has never happened for two reasons: (1) the spirit of the church has discerned that an ordained ministry be designated to lead the church in service (*diakonia*); and (2) deacons are quite politically aware. When Paul Van Buren retired in 2001 and Jimmy Carr was no longer leading the Section on Deacons, Anita Wood was chosen to join the staff of GBHEM. Wood was experienced in writing and monitoring legislation because of her previous work with the General Commission on the Status and Role of Women. Wood began working closely with any legislation coming from GBHEM or petitions that would affect the chapters in the *Discipline* relating to ministry. She was especially attuned to any petitions that would open the paragraphs on the ordained deacon. An informal network of deacons who had been elected as delegates, and other deacons who were influential in their annual conferences, could be alerted. They could then speak with the delegates and either support or warn against the petitions. Every four years, some petitions needed to be defeated. Wood recalls, "We overcame those. It's a good thing it's only every four years. When it came to it, we had enough strong deacon delegates."

In more than twenty years, no major changes have occurred. As Deacon David Dodge, who was assistant to the bishop in the Florida Conference for many years, says, "What we have been doing around our understanding of orders is tinkering—maybe fine tuning is a better term—maybe just tinkering."

Most of the tinkering has been related to the candidacy process. Efforts to shorten it for both deacons and elders have gained traction at times. The term *probationary* was changed to *provisional* in 2008. The argument was that *probation* carried the implication that one had done something wrong and needed to be returned to good status. The 1996 decision to name the entrance into this status as *commissioning* has stood the test of time. The provisional period begins with commissioning and continues until the candidate is ordained or discontinued.

When the paragraphs from the 1996 and 2016 *Disciplines* are examined side by side, the central concepts are almost unchanged, despite five General Conferences that could have made additions or deletions. The differences that emerged seem to respond to concerns of the moment. For instance, an addition to the section on qualifications for ordination for both deacons and elders states that the candidate must, "teach and model generous Christian giving with a focus on tithing as God's standard of giving" (¶304.1.c). Some delegates evidently believed that clergy were doing a poor job of teaching and practicing stewardship. Another addition directs every congregation to encourage a "culture of call." This perhaps indicates a concern that too few persons were experiencing a call to ministry (¶302; ¶303.4). Statistics were revealing that the average age of ordained elders was going up, and younger persons were not entering candidacy. Programs to address this challenge were funded and instigated along with these added sentences in the *Discipline*. These concerns were directed at elders and did not really alter the original concept of the deacon.

One change that has been especially helpful for deacons' sense of parity and ministry focus was added to ¶329. This change came out of the

2008–2012 Ministry Study, which included several deacons. Ever since 1996, deacons had been ordained to Word and service. Elders were ordained to Word, service, sacrament and order. In 2012, the words *compassion and justice* were added. Deacons "are ordained to Word, Service, Compassion, and Justice." The 2012 General Conference also added the sentence "The work of deacons is a work of justice, serving with compassion as they seek to serve those on the margins of society." These changes added more clarity about the distinctive focus of deacons.

Other legislation has opened the possibility for some deacons to offer the sacraments in their appointments. At the 2008 General Conference in Fort Worth, a sentence was added to ¶328 that made it possible (but difficult) to be granted sacramental authority. David Dodge was invited to be the presenter for the legislation. This is another dramatic story that reveals how the agenda and the presiding bishop can make space for legislation or not. If a petition does not come to the plenary for a vote, it simply dies. That nearly happened in this case. Dodge had been invited to present a legislative item that could extend sacramental privilege to deacons. He tells the story:

> I was up on the platform ready to present on Wednesday. They told me it might come up. And it didn't. So, they said I should be back here on Thursday. I was there, ready. And it didn't come up. I was back on Friday. I was there all day on Friday. It wasn't until Friday night [with the conference closing scheduled for midnight] that this piece came forward. The bishop hurried me along. I had already cut my speech way down. All in a rush to get out of there. It passed by 72 percent, despite a couple of arguments that were made on the floor.

In 1996, the supporters of the new deacon had relinquished the right to sacramental presidency in exchange for the support of some elders. In 2008, the General Conference was ready to walk that back to some extent. Paragraph 328, "The Ministry of a Deacon," contains this new sentence, "For the sake of extending the mission and ministry of the church, a pastor-in-charge or district superintendent may request that the bishop grant local sacramental authority to the deacon to administer the sacraments in the absence of an elder, within a deacon's primary appointment." A few deacons began to seek this authorization.[1] Some bishops saw the wisdom of it, especially for deacons appointed as chaplains or campus ministers. Other bishops were very resistant to granting this authority. Many arguments have gone on over this issue. Some believe that authorizing deacons for sacramental presidency blurs the line differentiating the two orders. Others believe that the sacraments and ordination go together. Deacons are ordained; they should be authorized to preside.

In 2016, the General Conference moved a bit closer. The 2016 *Book of Discipline* changes the sentence just a bit: "For the sake of extending the mission and ministry of the church and offering the means of grace to the world, the resident bishop of the annual conference in which the deacon is appointed may authorize the deacon to preside at the celebration of the sacraments" (¶328). This allows a deacon to speak directly to the bishop without needing a pastor-in-charge or district superintendent to initiate the request. In addition, the 2016 General Conferenced added another phrase, earlier in the paragraph: "or in presiding at the celebration of the sacraments when contextually appropriate and duly authorized." The paragraph now makes it clear that some deacons will be authorized for sacramental presidency. Chapter 8 will include a further discussion of the connection between sacraments and ordination.

Consolidation and Strengthening

The diaconal ministers and deacons on the staff of GBHEM have been important voices interpreting the order of deacon. They lead the way in connecting to the ecumenical diaconate. They have articulated the theology and functional place of the deacon in training sessions, print and media, and in their encouragement of candidates and deacons. Several times since 1996, they have sponsored convocations that gathered deacons from around the connection; those occasions have furthered the articulation of the concept of deacon. They offered formation events for provisional deacons, which prepared them for their interviews with the Board of Ordained Ministry and clarified the meaning of ordination. Books have been published. After 1996 (until the financial calamities following the sexuality debates that reduced resources for the general church agencies after 2016), deacons on the staff of GBHEM took the lead in interpreting to the denomination the need for and identity of the deacon.

Once the mad rush to organize and train conferences, bishops, district superintendents, boards of ordained ministry, and diaconal ministers for the first round of ordination services in 1997 was over, the Section of Deacons and Diaconal Ministers, which had become part of the Division of Ordained Ministry in 1996, turned back to the work of teaching the denomination about deacons. They worked with the GBHEM Office of Interpretation and with United Methodist Communications to produce print and other media that interpreted the ordained deacon. Joaquin Garcia recalls that the plan was to have a leading article every few months. Articles about deacons began showing up regularly in *The Circuit Rider, The Interpreter, Newscope, Connections, Colleague, The Quarterly Review,* and *Occasional Papers,* which were published by GBHEM.

The *Occasional Papers* were more scholarly explorations of issues related to the ordering of ministry. One of the first was released in 2002 by Robert Cummings Neville, then dean of the Boston University School of Theology. While including a skeptical perspective on the new deacon, Neville's paper also speaks of the value of the deacon. Neville points out that both deacons and elders are ordained to Word, but he suggests that *Word* has a different meaning for deacons. He says that deacons may not be as well trained as elders in biblical studies, but deacons may know more about the needs of the world to which the gospel speaks. When deacons read this paper, they understand that comparison, but Neville began that section by writing, "I conclude that the ministry of the Word mandated for deacons is simply not as serious with regard to responsibility for the Word as it is for elders" (9–10). The Neville paper raised some eyebrows.

Sondra Higgins Matthaei, a professor at Saint Paul School of Theology, contributed another paper in 2003. Her conclusion was, "The ministry of the deacon is a spiritual pilgrimage in servant leadership, a pilgrimage in which the Holy Spirit continues to call deacons into ever-deeper love for God and neighbor" (9). Matthaei, a Wesleyan scholar, connected the new deacon to Wesley and called it a "focused expression of social holiness" (8).

In 2007, I was invited to contribute another Occasional Paper, "The Promise of the United Methodist Order of Deacon in the Twenty-first Century: Partners with the Whole People of God." This piece was (no surprise) hopeful about the new order but also described some of the difficulties it was facing. I wrote, "Co-existing orders of ordained leaders—one more traditional and the other less bound by earlier models of pastor and parson— will be in creative tension as each offers its distinctive gifts to the church. The tension is most productive when power is equalized by ordination and full membership in the annual conference" (18). The publication of scholarly papers was contributing to the ongoing dialogue about the new order.

The Section of Deacons and Diaconal Ministry went to work on a book intended to be a resource for the new deacons and the church. New deacons would be the primary interpreters for the new order, and this book would be helpful for them. *The Deacon: Ministry Through Words of Faith and Acts of Love* by Paul E. Van Buren and Benjamin L. Hartley was published by GBHEM in 2000. It included a discussion of the historical and theological basis for the 1996 decision as well as stories that described, in practical terms, how deacons were finding and negotiating appointments. Deacons welcomed this book. It helped them address the constant request to explain themselves and their ministries.

GBHEM Associate General Secretary Jimmy Carr envisioned another new book for a broader audience. At the 1998 Convocation for United Methodist Deacons and Diaconal Ministers (October 22–25, 1998), Carr posed a question to a group of deacons and others who were teaching in seminaries and colleges. He asked this group of academics what they thought the new order needed. Some spoke enthusiastically about the ministry deacons were doing around the connection. Others thought that a book written by a deacon and an elder might be a good idea. Some thought that highlighting stories of deacons along with an informative and theological text would help the church to understand the new deacon. In the end, my husband, an elder, and I were asked to write the book. *A Deacon's Heart: The New United Methodist Diaconate* by Margaret Ann Crain and Jack L. Seymour was published in 2001 by Abingdon Press. The book received wide attention from deacons and candidates. People often report that they read the book and knew immediately that God was calling them to the order of deacon—they had a "deacon's heart."

The title caught on and has often been mentioned in gatherings of deacons. It came from an ecumenical gathering of people supporting diaconal ministries, which had been organized by Jimmy Carr and held at Garrett-Evangelical Theological Seminary. Four denominations and three deaconess communities were represented. A Lutheran woman, Nancy Gable, who directed a program for diaconal ministers proclaimed to the group, "From the moment I arrived here, I felt like we were a community. We share convictions and commitments. This happens every time I gather with deacons, deaconesses, and diaconal ministers. We share a 'deacon's heart'" (Crain 2001, 15). Indeed, that "deacon's heart" continues to resonate with deacons.

A second book on United Methodist deacons was published by Abingdon in 2014. This too would not have been published without the advocacy of Anita Wood, one of the deacons at GBHEM. Because editors feared it would not sell well, Abingdon Press would not agree to publish *The United Methodist Deacon Ordained to Word, Service, Compassion and Justice* until some funding was made available through GBHEM. In writing this second book, I attempted to speak from the standpoint of the now-established order of deacon. The book includes stories of deacons and their ministries. Publications such as these books have helped many who are discerning whether they might be called to ordained ministry as a deacon. Most who read the book report that either they immediately felt "this is me!" or they realized that it was not an identity they could embrace.

In addition to media and print resources, the GBHEM staff and members of the board knew that gatherings for formation and encouragement would be important. The plan was to hold a national gathering every four years. The first of these was held in Houston, Texas in 1998, with the theme: "In Celebration and Anticipation." Jimmy Carr gathered a design team that included eight deacons representing all five US jurisdictions of the church. Leaders were well known to deacons. Mary Elizabeth Moore, Cynthia Wilson, Rosemary Skinner Keller, and N. Lynne Westfield were some of the deacon presenters. Patty Meyers led the Bible studies. Jack Seymour and I spoke at a plenary about how the people of God raise and address issues of faith such as vocation, mission, justice, hope, and community as they live their faith in daily life—bridging church and world in living.[2] Deacons who attended found it formational and empowering. They were beginning to live into their new identity as ordained ministers. One deacon who attended that event still remembers how helpful a workshop on pensions and retirement was. Deacons were trying to understand their new relationship to the pension program of the denomination. Some of these folks had first been recognized as consecrated lay workers, then became consecrated diaconal ministers, and transitioned to ordained deacons in 1997. Robert Carlisle, who had experienced each office, describes the transitions as "a great ride."

One of the most memorable parts of the 1998 convocation was the "death of the church" service, complete with a casket borrowed from a local funeral home. A panel that included N. Lynne Westfield, Mary Elizabeth Moore, and Rosemary Skinner Keller challenged the group to reconsider their concept of *church*. They wanted participants to struggle with whether the church is a sacred building, an institution, or a mission and ministry. Then each participant was invited to write an answer to the question, "What needs to die in my understanding and to be born in the church and in me in order to step out boldly to fulfill my calling?" Patty Meyers describes the powerful worship ritual that followed:

> I borrowed a casket from a local Houston Funeral Service. Ardis Letey created banners; we had a band, and we also had one of the Black college choirs as our guests. There was a New Orleans style funeral procession from the back of the ballroom to the casket in front. The choir sang a dirge, and each participant placed in the casket what they believed had to die in order for the Church to live. Then, true to the New Orleans style return from the cemetery, the band played, and everyone sang, "When the Saints Go Marching In" to celebrate resurrection for the Church!

Many deacons who were there can still remember this service.

Another convocation for deacons and diaconal ministers was held in 2003 in Dallas. Its theme was "Connecting the Church with the World and the World with the Church." Rev. Grace Imathiu led the Bible study, and Barbara Day Miller designed and coordinated the rich worship times. Deacons, deaconesses, and diaconal ministers came from Norway, Mozambique, Liberia, Philippines, Brazil, and Lithuania. It was a global gathering with nearly six hundred participants! The biblical text undergirding the convocation was from Isaiah 43:1-2: "I have called you by name; you are mine. . . . I will be with you." General Secretary Jerome King Del Pino urged the group to radicalize *diakonia* so that it would become "something more than another layer of maintenance leadership in a church that already has too many layers" (*Colleague* Summer/Fall 2003, 13). The gathered deacons were unsettled by his comment. They knew they were already expanding and living the call of deacon.

Joaquin Garcia was part of a panel about the future of the diaconate. His statement listed three stages that he believed would be necessary for positive change:

1. To formulate a vision that will capture and give direction to people's hopes for a diaconate that will incarnate their call to serve.

The church will be challenged to go beyond its conventional wisdom and stretch its thinking about an ordering of ministry that is open and can move beyond the limits of what we already know and understand.

2. To gather support through the formation of networks and coalitions to embody that vision for ministry.

3. To gain momentum, faith, and hope in order to bring the vision to fruition even during hard and frustrating times.

Garcia urged the deacons to read the signs of the times and shape their ministries accordingly. The event began with an ice storm but ended with deacons inspired to connect world and church.

In 2007, deacons travelled to Orlando, Florida for a convocation. Deacons Adrienne Ann Ilsemann and Debby Fox were the design chairs. This four-day event was held in a resort that featured a large green area with many small bridges. Ilsemann and Fox realized right away what a perfect setting this would be for deacons, whose role is to bridge church and world. They provided a guide for participants to do a prayer walk using the bridges as tangible places to consider their ministry as a bridge between church and world. On the walk, deacons were invited to consider what it means to be a bridge. More than that, the event was held *in* an oasis and *was* an oasis. Deacons often face confusion everywhere they turn and grow weary of constantly having to explain what a deacon is. Ilsemann wanted deacons to come together in this oasis and celebrate: "Come on home! It is so sweet to cultivate a space where we are together."

The design team was challenged to find a way to support Project Tariro, a new mission project that would empower unemployed Zimbabweans with HIV/AIDS and their caregivers. Paul Van Buren was leading the project. The call went out to deacons across the church to begin to raise money for Tariro and bring it to the convocation. Some deacons held bake sales. Other deacons asked their bishops for funds. Deacons raised money from many sources. And somehow, when the offering was collected in Orlando, more than $44,000 was there! Project Tariro, a mission project of deacons, was off the ground! Debby Fox remembers the piles of money; she spent hours in a little room counting. It felt like a revival!

Five seminary students traveled to that convocation with me. All but one of them are now deacons. Adrienne Stricker, who is co-chair of the order in her conference, remembers that the convocation affirmed and deepened her call. She could see how she could make a difference in the world through the order of deacons: "I felt embraced by people who were deep theological explorers." The conversations were rich. Stricker recalls:

> At the very end, this is a silly moment, I remember because I was with Jenny. We all lined up in this huge circle all around the room. We all started doing a leg kick thing to "This Little Light of Mine." And I remember thinking, Wow! This is beautiful. It was a silly moment, but it felt freeing in some way. It felt like these are my people.

These are my people. Perhaps that is why the convocations were so valuable as the new order found its way in the church.

The banner created for that event by Amanda McElray Hunter remains one of the most beloved images for deacons. It has four large panels, each with a pitcher and basin. Many deacons have these images in their offices, and it remains at the heading of the United Methodist Deacon Facebook group page. The pitcher and basin are associated with Jesus washing the disciples' feet, the archetype of *diakonia.* The convocation of 2007 was the last large gathering of deacons to date. Three large convocations in the first ten years were significant sources of identity formation and encouragement for the new deacons.

Joaquin Garcia reports that, in 2007, there were 1,381 active deacons; 213 retired. In candidacy that year were an additional 1,659. To have six hundred gather for the convocation was a testament to their commitment to one another and to the order of deacons.

Mission Caravans

Between 1995 and 2003, six caravans for peace were led by UMC deacons. Joaquin Garcia was very committed to these caravans because of their potential to stretch the prophetic imagination and knowledge of deacons. The trips were always cross-cultural; they provided a creative dislocation for those who participated. After the first trip to Sarajevo, other groups traveled to Cuba, Bolivia, Haiti, Sand Mountain in Alabama, and Chicago. After the successful fundraising at the 2007 Convocation, another group traveled to Zimbabwe to visit Project Tariro.

Each trip gathered a diverse group of deacons and brought them to a place of deep need that they had never experienced before. They were then asked to write reflections that could be shared widely. This program was another way to address the need for diversity both in those who were part of the Order of Deacon and in deacons' understanding of the needs of the world. They also embodied the deacons' call to connect the church with the world and the world to the church.

Organizing the Order of Deacons

In the 1996 *Book of Discipline*, a new section III, "Clergy Orders in The United Methodist Church," contained four new paragraphs. Paragraph 311 declared, "There shall be in each annual conference an Order of Deacons and an Order of Elders." All ordained full members of an annual conference were to participate in their appropriate order. These orders were defined as covenant communities that would "mutually support, care for, and hold accountable its members." Paragraph 312 listed activities that the orders were to undertake such as "continuing formation in relationship to Jesus Christ through such experiences as Bible study, study of issues facing the church and society, and theological exploration in vocational identity and leadership." Other phrases in that paragraph point to ways to nurture relationships that both support and hold people accountable. The Order was to relate to the Board of Ordained Ministry but did not have a supervisory or evaluative role.

The Orders were convened by the resident bishop in each conference. The board nominated someone within the Order to serve as chairperson for the quadrennium, and the Order then elected that person. The activities of the Order were to be funded by the board. Paragraph 314 ended with, "Acceptance of the status of full membership will constitute a commitment to regular participation in the life of the Order." Most of the deacons ordained in 1997 accepted this commitment with joy, for they had come through the crucible of denominational discernment and were deeply connected to one another in their new identity.

Joaquin Garcia went right to work helping the Orders find their way. He began the practice of providing events for chairs of all the orders to get together to share ideas and clarify their responsibilities. By 2002, Garcia's records indicate that most conferences had an Order of Deacons that was vital and active. They encouraged and recruited candidates who were experiencing a call to the ministry of the deacon, held retreats in the annual conference for sabbath and renewal, lifted up the Order of Deacons in the annual conference, and met annually with their resident bishop. With the sustained support of GBHEM, the orders began to function well.

As already noted, the idea of an "Order" for ordained elders and deacons was new. When it was passed in 1996, the hope was that the Orders would provide spiritual formation and fellowship. For elders, it was not such a good fit. Of course, there were, and still are, far more elders than deacons in each conference, so those groups were much larger. Their spiritual fellowship had traditionally been the annual conference in which they held their membership. As the annual conference begins each year, United Methodists belt out "And Are We Yet Alive?" with tears threatening to escape because it feels like a homecoming, especially for ordained persons who are not members of a congregation but members of the annual conference. The Order seemed like another meeting to attend, an unnecessary obligation. In many annual conferences, the Order of Deacons continues to have retreats and other gatherings that are valued by their participants.

Formation Events During the Provisional Period

GBHEM staff in the Section on Deacons continued to take the lead in interpreting and advocating for the order of deacon, although the personnel was changing. Both Jack Harnish and Jimmy Carr left the staff in 2002. Joaquin Garcia became assistant general secretary, and Sharon Rubey followed Joaquin as director of Conference Relations and Candidacy. Paul Van Buren retired in 2001.

In 2001, Anita Wood came on the staff as director of Professional Ministry Development, the last person hired by Ireson. Because of her previous work with the General Commission on the Status and Role of Women and her experience in writing and monitoring legislation, she was given added responsibilities and began working closely with the legislation coming from GBHEM in preparation for the 2004 General Conference. She also watched for petitions that addressed the ministry paragraphs.

The staff had been reorganized to reflect the change in orders. Both Sharon Rubey and Joaquin Garcia of the Section on Deacons continued and expanded the work of supporting deacon candidates and training the chairs of the orders and boards of ordained ministry. In addition to offering training events and publishing handbooks for these conference level officers, they began offering a formation event nearly every year. Provisional deacons in all conferences were encouraged to attend a formation event before they applied for ordination. These events, like the one put together for diaconal ministers transitioning to deacon, were times to consider call, learn about appointments, and consolidate one's identity. Formation events were especially valuable for provisional deacons who were in conferences with few deacons. They needed the support, information, and challenge that the formation events offered. They needed to meet other deacons. Those provisional deacons who attended the formation events came back more prepared for their ordination interviews and convinced of their call to the order of deacon. By October of 1998, the newsletter *Colleague* reported that nine formation events had been held and more than 1,700 persons had attended them (Winter/Spring 1999, 14). These events have continued to be offered. In recent years, however, they have often been linked to other gatherings of deacons, and they risk becoming diluted or discontinued.

General Secretary Roger Ireson had written, "We have chosen to emphasize for a new century that ministry is collaborative and have symbolized this in the single ordination to deacon and elder while at the same time giving emphasis to the ministry of the laity" (*Colleague* Summer/Fall 1996, 3). Just a few years later, the new general secretary, Dr. Jerome Del Pino, an outspoken opponent of the legislation, wrote in *Colleague* that "Orders in the church right now don't make sense theologically or ecclesiologically" (Summer/Fall 2002, 5).

Joaquin Garcia retired in 2003. Garcia had been there twenty-five years and had seen the growth of diaconal ministry into the vision of a full and equal order of deacon. Then the General Board of Higher Education and Ministry restructured and eliminated the three Ministry Sections.

Deacons Claim Their Voice

The first step toward the permanent ordained diaconate was the recognition of the consecrated lay worker, which emerged as part of the formation of The United Methodist Church in 1968. The justification at that historic moment was not so much theological as it was an attempt to create more just employment for professionals employed in the church. The new ecclesiology and the polity did not quite match up. R. Harold Hipps was energetic and persuasive and, along with others, he led the effort to get the office of consecrated lay worker approved by the new denomination. But the idea that the church needed permanent diaconal leaders was already percolating ecumenically and in the new denomination. Lay worker and Christian educator, Rena Yocom, was part of the earliest discussions (beginning in 1970) in the board of the new General Board of Higher Education and Ministry and in the Ministry Study Commissions. She asked, "Is there no ecclesial affirmation for *my* call?" That question was a catalyst driving the conversation from 1970 until 1996. The 1970 group was encouraged to take her question seriously by lay members who argued that their lives were ministry. Elders on the staff of GBHEM were supportive too and aware of the growing ecumenical consensus that the deacon should hold a distinctive place in Christian ministry.

After Rosalie Bentzinger was hired to run the Division of Diaconal Ministry, advocating for ecclesial affirmation of *diakonia* was accelerated and organized by Bentzinger and her staff, Joaquin Garcia and Paul Van Buren. Diaconal ministers and their allies also helped the whole church to see the possibilities in the permanent diaconate. Each quadrennium, persons were elected to serve as directors of the Division of Diaconal Ministry, and they too became convinced of the need for that ecclesial affirmation. The Diaconal Clearness Committee that wrote the legislation affirmed by the 1996 General Conference was all diaconal ministers. From one, Rena Yocom, who spoke up in a Ministry Study Commission, the voices had multiplied and become more effective in their advocacy.

Meanwhile, the voices of established historians and theologians in the denomination remained resistant. Richard Heitzenrater, quoted in earlier chapters, was unconvinced. Thomas E. Frank, whose book on polity became the standard for many seminary courses, was initially lukewarm to the idea. Dennis Campbell, from Duke Divinity School, was not an ally during the 1992 presentation to the General Conference. Dale Dunlap, professor from Saint Paul School of Theology, was a convert, but he started out thinking a permanent deacon was a bad idea. Jack Harnish had fought the idea as a General Conference delegate but changed his mind later as he worked with Jimmy Carr to implement the General Conference action. Jerome King Del Pino, who served as general secretary of GBHEM (2001–2010), was never satisfied with the General Conference's decision. He stated, "I never was opposed to the permanent order of deacon per se but to the proposal because it was being planted with one hand tied behind its back. Had the church said, we are committed to this order, [it would be different], but basically economics has driven the mission." Del Pino notes that the Council of Bishops has never claimed the Order of Deacon: "Bishops don't want to have anything to do with empowering and enabling the annual conference to provide enough money to ensure that deacons are doing justice. I wish that every conference could claim they've got deacons who are assigned to city councils or state legislatures. Or, [be able to claim] we've got deacons appointed to be in the public square and in the centers of power where the questions of justice are addressed." Del Pino's vision of the Order harmonizes with the language of the *Discipline*, but he has also identified the conflict between the vision and the reality.

Many deacons were waiting for the scholars and church leaders to affirm their identity, but it never materialized. As Del Pino sees it, "Deacons have had to spend their life dealing with a system that really did not want it. Everybody in their respective silos basically said, that's not my problem." Painful as it is, Del Pino has offered an apt description of the situation that deacons face in the UMC. Some historians were publicly regretting the departure from the Anglican practice of sequential ordination. Theologians were concerned about an ordained office that was disconnected from sacrament. Because sacraments were not connected to ordination for the new deacon, a new definition of *ordination* was necessary. And deacons were not itinerating, which was a cherished part of the Methodist way of attending to its mission to "spread scriptural holiness across the land," an often-quoted phrase that originated with John Wesley. The Council of Bishops never appeared to be interested in the Order of Deacon, perhaps because deacons were not itinerating in the same way as elders and bishops had only partial power over their appointments. Many highly respected scholars and leaders did not support the action of 1996. In fact, it was called a "debacle" and a "disaster" more than once.

Deacons stepped into the gap and began to speak for themselves. They had been doing it all along, of course. They spoke when they described their divine call to ordained ministry. Many who experienced a call found themselves justifying and explaining constantly. Boards of Ordained Ministry ask a candidate, why do you need to be ordained to do this work? The ultimate answer is, God has called me to do this ministry as an ordained deacon. Candidates have to define the deacon and justify its existence in their interviews. Elders never have to justify the existence of their order. Many deacons have an extra burden of explanation as they seek affirmation of their call. While some deacons work in churches as educators, musicians, administrators, and youth pastors; deacons also work in the world as teachers, chaplains, lawyers, therapists, professors, spiritual directors, wellness coaches, yoga instructors, nurses, directors of nonprofits, and in a myriad of other settings for ministry.

Deacon Dialogues and the Ecumenical Network for the Diaconate

One of the settings where deacons were claiming their voices was seminaries. All of the United Methodist seminaries responded to the General Conference action. Most found someone who could assist students who might be called to the deacon track to find the courses they needed and to locate mentors as they worked through the candidacy processes in their home conference. Garrett-Evangelical Theological Seminary's President Neal Fisher responded to the 1996 General Conference decision by creating a faculty position to support students preparing for the new order of deacon. In 1997, I was hired as assistant professor of Christian Education and director of Deacon Studies. I became academic advisor for any student who enrolled in Deacon Studies. This was a program that met the educational requirements for ordination through a set of courses called the Basic Graduate Theological Studies and a professional certification. Deacon Studies were an alternative to the three-year Master of Divinity or other master's level theological degree that could also meet the requirements. At first, the students who came to the Deacon Studies program were often second career. They were nervous about taking courses alongside students in the degree programs, but most soon discovered that they could hold their own academically, and they loved learning about theology, Bible, church history, and the other basic courses. Time after time, a new student would try a Deacon Studies course because he or she was hired by a congregation to run children's ministry or as a youth ministry leader. Eventually, many of those students completed a Master's degree and were ordained as deacons. Garrett-Evangelical administrators and faculty actively supported the new order as did other seminaries.

While deacon candidates were attending classes, they shared their call stories with one another and with other students. They also learned from each other about how to organize ministry in a congregation or how to start a nonprofit organization. Most important, they often confirmed a call to ordination. The gatherings of Deacon Studies students were usually enriched by a visit from GBHEM's Anita Wood, who could answer their questions about ordination processes. She also brought the print materials interpreting the deacon to the denomination. These were carried home and used to help educate the pastor in charge and the Staff Parish Relations Committee about deacons. GBHEM was offering scholarship support for tuition. All these supports encouraged candidates and made it possible for many to pursue a call to ordination. Students in the degree programs were also responding to a call to ordination as deacons and were part of the Deacon Studies gatherings.

After a few years of interaction with these creative, spiritual, enthusiastic persons who had experienced a call to ministry, the Garrett-Evangelical Deacon Studies program began sponsoring events called Deacon Dialogues. The publicity for a Dialogue in April 2005 stated, "United Methodist deacons need to speak clearly to the church about who we are and what God has called us to do. The Deacon Dialogue event will provide an opportunity to meet together, hear from some of our most articulate deacons, and share in the efforts to clarify, for The United Methodist Church, the unique contribution of deacons to the mission of Jesus Christ." The Deacon Dialogue program in 2005 included Jimmy Carr, Jack Harnish, Rena Yocom, Joaquin Garcia, Diane Eberhart, Nan Zoller, Rosemary Skinner Keller, Anita Wood, Sharon Rubey, Patty Meyers, Julie Hagar Love, Deanna Stickley-Miner, and many others. It was a Who's Who of people who had been part of the journey to 1996 and beyond. The program included a discussion about deacons and elders in team ministry, the meaning of ordination, sacrament and the deacon, and the meaning of conference membership. It was a heady gathering, attracting participants from all jurisdictions and many conferences.

Another Deacon Dialogue in 2007 brought more than one hundred thirty-five deacons from forty-six annual conferences to Garrett for more conversation. Ten of those who attended had been elected as delegates to the 2008 General Conference. Another Dialogue was held in 2009, and Deacon Dialogue III occurred in 2010. Deacon Dialogues highlighted the particular focus of deacons' ministry and the theological basis for the order. Garrett-Evangelical has offered leadership to the denomination as it provided a venue for deacons to claim their voice.[3]

Concurrently, through Garrett-Evangelical, I was also administering and leading an organization with an ecumenical membership: The Ecumenical Network for the Diaconate. This organization began because Jimmy Carr had sponsored a gathering of leaders from the ecumenical diaconate at Garrett-Evangelical. Ten representatives of different faith communities with some form of diaconal ministry attended. (This was the meeting that generated the phrase, *a deacon's heart*, which became the title of the book I co-authored about the UMC deacon.) Attending this meeting were an Episcopal archdeacon, the president of the Lutheran Deaconess Association, a deaconess from the United Methodist Deaconess office at the General Board of Global Ministry in New York, a woman who directed the educational program for Evangelical Lutheran Church in American diaconal ministers, and many others.

As they all shared their calling to diaconal work, they found that they were deeply connected in their commitments. When they described how they operated within their denominations, they discovered great differences. The conversation was rich and encouraging. Out of that meeting came a network that continued for more than a dozen years. The Roman Catholic deacons and their vicar joined soon after the group was formed; the Archdiocese of Chicago had more than five hundred deacons at that time. The Ecumenical Network for the Diaconate met once or twice a year and learned from one another over about twelve years. Deacons and deaconesses from the Chicago area participated as did national leaders from the churches. The conversation continued to highlight differences in how people were employed as well as revealing an inspiring common commitment to *diakonia*.

Ecumenical gatherings of diaconal workers have been going on for a long time. These ecumenical conversations have been empowering and encouraging for participants. After the Industrial Revolution, a deaconess movement flourished in Germany in response to the social ills resulting from urbanization. The German deaconesses were mostly nurses and teachers connected to the German Lutheran Church. They lived together in a mother house. Eventually, this movement spread across the globe. Today, that movement, along with many other expressions of the diaconate, gathers as DIAKONIA World Federation. United Methodist deacons are members of DIAKONIA and send representatives to the quadrennial gatherings. They are also members of Diakonia of the Americas and Caribbean (DOTAC), which includes Protestant diaconal folks from Canada to the southern end of South America. Deacon Joaquin Garcia was instrumental in getting DOTAC chartered as a not-for-profit corporation in the United States so that it could receive contributions. UMC deacons are part of DOTAC, and some attend its meetings.

Deaconesses in the UMC (and home missioners, their male counterparts) are part of this ecumenical diaconal group too because, of course, they are part of the larger worldwide *diakonia*. Deaconesses are commissioned and appointed by bishops. The office for deaconesses is located with United

Methodist Women. The ecumenical groups include many forms of diaconal ministry around the world. Attending one of these events is a thrilling potpourri of languages, dress, and culture, but the commonality of commitment to service shines through.

When a United Methodist deacon interacts in these ecumenical diaconal groups, it soon becomes apparent that the parity with presbyters (elders) that United Methodist deacons enjoy is not present in other churches. Most deacons, diaconal ministers, and deaconesses are educated in separate programs and places from their presbyters, which reveals their second-class status. Most do not share in the polity as equals. Many are asked to do their diaconal ministry as volunteers; a sense of professional identity is not encouraged. Roman Catholic deacons are authorized to offer all but two of the church's seven sacraments, but only men are eligible. If they are married, their wives attend classes alongside the future deacon and must signify their support in writing. All of these differences emphasize the amazingly strong proposal that was approved by the 1996 General Conference. And thankfully, General Conference has only tinkered with it since then.

This chapter began with the uncertainty of how the new order of deacon would develop and gain acceptance. In the decades since its creation in 1996, the deacons themselves have answered that uncertainty over and over with their voices and their ministries. Both in the church and in the world, deacons bring compassion to their work as they seek to make the world more just. Deacons serve the church at its highest levels of leadership as well as the most vulnerable citizens in homeless shelters and hospice care. The boundaries have continued to expand as deacons have explained to their bishops how God has called them and equipped them for a particular appointment. New fields of endeavor and powerful cultural movements have drawn deacons into many settings. And yet, the promise of the deacon is not fully realized in the UMC.

8 After 25 Years, What Is a Deacon?

The church is not a building, the church is not a steeple,
the church is not a resting place, the church is a people.

—Richard K. Avery and Donald S. Marsh (*UMH*, 558)

In the 1960s, the concept of *ministry* and the role of laity began to shift for Methodists. As laity claimed their vocation to love God and their neighbors, all aspects of their lives became potential places to live that out. Evidence of the shift is that the term *ministry,* formerly understood to be the exclusive domain of ordained clergy, was redefined as the work of all Christians. Following conversations at the World Council of Churches, we began to speak about baptism as the call to vocation for all Christians. Earlier chapters of this book have traced this change, which was completed by the General Conference of 1984. That major shift was made more concrete by the decision to expand the ordained leadership of the denomination to include a group of ordained leaders whose focus was on equipping the people of God for ministry in their daily lives: the deacon.

This creative and courageous decision means that two distinct and complementary types of ordained persons are available to help lead the mission of the church. The elder is ordained to Word, service, sacrament, and order. The deacon is ordained to Word, service, compassion, and justice. The elder is an extension of the traditional parish pastor. The deacon is a new order focused on extending the ministry of God's people throughout the community and world. Along with their theological expertise, deacons are persons with specialized skills whose ministry bridges church and world.

The two orders are appointed differently. Elders itinerate to a "missional appointment" and are appointed annually by the bishop. Deacons must find a place to contribute to the mission of the church and then seek the bishop's approval and appointment. Elders are expected to move from congregation to congregation whenever asked; in turn, they are guaranteed an appointment. With the new deacon, the bishop does not initiate the move, and there is no guarantee that the deacon will find one. The deacon is a departure from tradition, and the church has slowly and partially lived into the possibilities it presents.

What is a deacon? Now that nearly a quarter century has passed since the contemporary embodiment of *diakonia* was embraced by the General Conference, what does it actually look like? The order has evolved. It has survived constant legislative efforts to enhance and to discontinue it. Despite that constant uncertainty, people have heard God calling them to ministry and found that the order of deacon best embodies that call. Lots of deacons have been ordained. Deacons have served in an ever widening variety of places with a huge range of skills and professions. It has been twenty-five years; some deacons have retired. Years of ministry by faithful deacons have revealed the power in the granting of ecclesial authorization for this work of Word, service, compassion, and justice.

The United Methodist Church, like all institutions, needs leaders to keep it on track to fulfill its mission. When you begin with the mission of this institution, both deacons and elders have a place in leadership. The mission of the church is "to make disciples of Jesus Christ for the transformation of the world" (*Discipline*, ¶120). Deacons, with their ordination to Word, service, compassion, and justice, are positioned to attend to the transformation of the world. The Study of Ministry report prepared for the 2020[2022] General Conference states that "deacons help the church love the world with the compassionate heart of Jesus and confront the powers of the world" as they reach out to those who are vulnerable or marginalized and help them create a more just and compassionate world (2020, 1013–1014). Also, when they are assisting at the altar with the sacraments during a local church worship service, deacons are a reminder of the needs of the world. Elders, of course, are also concerned with the transformation of the world, just as deacons contribute to the order of the church. But the primary focus of each order is distinct.

Appointing leaders with a different focus or a different role is not a new thing for the people called Methodist. Frederick Norwood, an eminent historian of the Methodist movement in the United States, wrote in 1960, that the "amazing success of the circuit rider would have been impossible without the unpublicized help of the local preacher, exhorter, and class leader" (35). Norwood saw the demise of circuit riders as the cause of the diminishment of local leaders. "The day had arrived," wrote Norwood, "when the people could sit back and say, 'Let the preacher do it'" (54). The conceptualization of the ordained deacon was careful to avoid this pitfall when it described the deacon as "leading and equipping the people of God" rather than as doing the church's ministry in the world.

Some additions to the *Discipline* over the last twenty years appear to make the link between ministry and the mission of the church more explicit for both deacons and elders. One added sentence in ¶305 states, "Those called to the ministry of deacon are called to witness to the Word in their words and actions, and to embody and lead the community's service in the world for the sake of enacting God's compassion and justice." Similarly, a sentence was added later in the same paragraph that relates the ministry of elders to the wider mission of the church. It says that elders are "to bear authority and responsibility to preach and teach the Word, to administer the sacraments, and to order the life of the church so it can be faithful in making disciples of Jesus Christ for the transformation of the world." Notice that the relationship to *Word* is nuanced for each order. Elders are to preach and teach, while deacons are to witness to the Word in their words and actions. Of course, deacons do preach and teach, and elders do witness to the Word in their words and actions. It is difficult to draw a line separating the ministry of the two orders because they overlap, but these sentences help to articulate the focus of ministry for each order and define how they complement each other.

How they complement each other becomes especially fuzzy when you try to distinguish by function or location. That approach has led to misunderstanding and inequality. It just doesn't work to say that deacons work in the world, and elders work in the church. Both deacons and elders may be appointed to church ministries; both deacons and elders may hold appointments that place their work primarily in the world. For too long, the shorthand distinction has been that elders do sacrament and deacons cannot. In fact, some deacons are now authorized to preside over sacraments. The *Discipline* now states, "For the sake of extending the mission and ministry of the church and offering the means of grace to the world, the resident bishop of the annual conference in which the deacon is appointed may authorize the deacon to preside at the celebration of the sacraments" (2016, ¶328). Over the more than twenty years since 1996, many questions about the relationship between deacons and elders have been raised and clarified. The difference is not function; it is not sacramental presidency; it is not in accountability to the church. It is in call, identity, and service.

Many times, I have listened to a person trying to discern what a spiritual stirring or unrest might mean. They often express it as a negative: "I don't want to be a pastor of a church." The stirring is a yearning to make a difference in the world, to address the needs of God's people through a specialized skill or interest. For instance, one young person has a journalism degree along with a theological degree and has used those skills to write and educate about inequities in the food supply. Another person took on some of the superstores in her community and advocated for more just employment practices. Another person has written a book on raising antiracist children. Other deacons have used community-organizing skills to start new faith communities. Several deacons are educators, fighting bullying and other injustices in their schools. Each of these deacons was moved by compassion and called to transform a situation into something more just.

The distinction is also clarified when we look at identity. The sentence from ¶305 quoted above is one helpful way to think about identity for deacons. "Deacons are called to witness to the Word in their words and actions, and to embody and lead the community's service in the world for the sake of enacting God's compassion and justice." These are actions—witness, embody, lead—but they flow from an identity. The report of the 2017–2020 Study of Ministry defines *ordination* as "an embodied posture of service and an enfleshed participation in the sublime movement of Spirit" (2020, 1005). The choices of *enfleshed* and *embodied* are powerful words suggesting that these are about *who* you are, not *what* you do. This incarnational language relates more to identity than to function.

Elders have a detailed job description in the *Discipline.* Paragraph 340 fills four pages with tasks for the elder, organized around the four foci of ordination: Word, service, sacrament, and order. Some of it is specific, such as the requirement to visit in homes or to administer the sacraments. Some sections are more general, such as the one about administering the education program of the congregation. This is a job description that would be appropriate for almost any elder who is appointed to a congregation. It differs from the paragraphs for deacons, which name general missional tasks such as to "exemplify and lead the church in servanthood" (¶305; see also ¶¶328–329).

As the Boards of Ordained Ministry and bishops have authorized, ordained, and appointed deacons over the years, the range of appointments that deacons hold has broadened. Deacons serve as doctors, lawyers, teachers, counselors, professors, chaplains, journalists, social workers, journalists, community organizers, administrators, musicians, therapists, nurses, artists, yoga instructors, missionaries, and more. Deacons are also employed in the church at all levels and in a wide range of positions, including as church planters. The list of appointments for deacons in every conference journal is a testimony to the ongoing expansion of understanding about who deacons are and what they do. These wide-ranging lists of places where deacons are appointed bump up against the stereotype of a clergyperson or minister as a local pastor or parish priest. For centuries, pastoral ministry or supervision of pastoral ministry (think bishop or pope) has been the primary, if not the only, definition of *clergy*. The idea that a person might be ordained to be a teacher, social worker, or lawyer is very new. Yet ordained United Methodist deacons are working in these professions and many other fields as well.

The 2020 Study of Ministry report contains these words: "The church participates boldly and humbly in God's mission in the world. This mission is not ours to create" (1007). The order of deacon is predicated on this understanding; they have discerned that God is calling them to bring compassion and justice to places where God is leading them in mission. "The Church exists for the sake of the world's transformation, and as such does not stand apart from the world" (1007). As this book is being written, the Spirit is leading us to dismantle White privilege and embrace a new way of being where Black Lives Matter and all people have what they need to thrive. Many deacons are speaking out and teaching the church about its systemic racism and leading change. Deacons embody this transformative hope of the church and offer their energy and expertise in search of that hope.

In the twenty-five years since the first diaconal ministers were ordained as deacons, many more have joined their ranks. At first, most deacons were employed by congregations. Some were also employed as conference staff or in general church agencies. But the diaconal ministers who advocated for the ordained deacon from 1976 to 1996 had a bigger idea. And as the church has lived into this new order, it has expanded. More and more deacons are now employed outside the local church. In 2020, the Northern Illinois Conference, with forty active deacons, reported that fifteen were appointed to congregations, and twenty-five were appointed beyond the local church. This is a significant shift from the beginnings, which were driven primarily by efforts to recognize the professionals serving congregations as Christian educators and musicians. Boards of Ordained Ministry in many conferences have recognized the value of leaders who bring the enfleshed Word to their work for compassion and justice in the world and the needs of the world back to the church. However, when an individual expresses a call to a profession that the Board of Ordained Ministry sees as unorthodox, that individual still needs to convince the interviewers that this is a place where the church can join with what God is already doing in the world. Sometimes, this process can be discouraging and difficult.

One woman who discerned a call to work on her family farm and make it a place for children to learn the wonder of God's creation faced resistance when she requested ordination as a deacon. Eventually, she was able to articulate her ministry clearly enough that the board approved her for commissioning. She is now teaching large groups of children every year about the cycle of the seasons, the ecological value of farmland, and the interrelatedness of all God's wondrous creation. Her ministry embodies Word, compassion, and justice.

When candidates meet with the Board of Ordained Ministry, they are often asked, "Why do you need to be ordained to do this?" In the case of the deacon appointed to her family farm, that was asked repeatedly. The answer is that God called her to ordination. She is appointed by her bishop to this ministry and accountable to the church. She is also teaching the church about the fragility of God's amazing diverse creation and helping the church to find ways to live more in harmony with the whole of creation. It is different to work on your farm as a mission of the church.

Still Unresolved, but Continuing to Respond to God's Call

Part of the reason that ordination as a deacon to work in a secular profession is not widely understood is that deacons are not yet a critical mass in The United Methodist Church. Some research seems to suggest that a group within a larger group can begin to exert influence when they reach about 20 percent of the total. A report from the General Commission on the Status and Role of Women claimed that deacons were 5 percent of all clergy (Ruch-Teegarden 2019). "All clergy" included licensed local pastors who are not ordained, so that statistic is a bit misleading. The same article reported that 17.4 percent of provisional clergy were deacons, indicating that the percentage is rising. Provisional clergy would include only candidates for deacon and elder. In 2020, a count of reports from annual conferences found only 1,424 ordained deacons and 327 provisional deacons (Statistics provided by Meg Lassiat via email correspondence). Perhaps in another ten years, deacons will become a critical mass. Until then, too many United Methodists have not yet seen or known a deacon and have had no reason to learn about them. Nevertheless, young people continue to respond positively to the idea of becoming a deacon. At the event for young United Methodists, "Exploration," a significant portion of attendees have indicated that they want to know more about serving as deacons. That is encouraging.

However, deacons choose a challenging road economically. Too many deacons have difficulty finding employment and end up on "transitional leave," the official status for unemployed clergy. Much of this is due to the shrinkage happening in mainline Protestant denominations. Fewer and smaller churches mean that the employment opportunities in specialized ministries such as Christian education and music ministry are shrinking too. More deacons must find a place for their ministry outside of the local church. Elders in good standing are guaranteed a full-time appointment; some deacons have found the order of elder is a better place to live out their calling and have transitioned to the order of elder or licensed local pastor. And yet, the theology of the denomination still supports the need for both ordained deacons and elders. Deacons are seeking out courses in nonprofit management and entrepreneurship to help them establish the ministries that God has put in their hearts. The strength and endurance these deacons demonstrate as they create a way to address a need is inspiring. As the Study of Ministry report indicates, "In every age and time, the people of God need leadership to navigate the tension between the Reign of God announced by Christ and the petty fiefdoms of this world in which human will and desire still hold sway" (2020, 1010). Clearly, the deacon who is ordained to Word, service, compassion, and justice has a role in this task!

Along with the passion that many deacons bring to their calling, they still must justify their ordination and their place in the church's structure.

The inconsistencies and contradictions in United Methodist polity are sometimes highlighted by the existence of the deacon. Rena Yocom wrote,

> [T]he understanding United Methodists have for ministry includes at least two "parent" informing traditions: the highly structured, reformed catholic view of the Church of England and the evangelical movement in which Wesley himself participated, which was characterized by the "extraordinary" ministry of preaching by unordained men and women. (Yocom 1991, 81)

Indeed, the most vigorous objections to the new order of deacon and elimination of sequential ordination for elders were based on its departure from the organization and practices of the Church of England in the time of John Wesley. At the same time, Wesley's creative methods of reaching out beyond the walls of the church building provide a precedent for an ordained deacon who represents, leads, and equips the church for its ministry in the world. The deacon and those who respond to a call to the work of a deacon are constantly disrupting the church and easy stereotypes of what it means to be ordained.

One of the reasons that every ministry study has struggled with the connection of ordination and sacraments is that the deacon is there, reminding them that not all who ordained are authorized. When that is held up to the troubling practice of authorizing laypersons for sacramental presidency when they are simply licensed and appointed for a year, the inconsistency is glaring. Boards of Ordained Ministry and General Conference clergy delegates tend to be mature elders and scholars, who were formed in their youth by the tradition. Many of them would be uncomfortable giving deacons full authorization for sacrament. Thus, the strange, inconsistent practice continues. Every ministry study so far has identified it as a problem.

Deacons continue to surprise and challenge the church to see the places that need healing, feeding, or the restoration of justice. The deacon appointed to a church near me is a very skillful musician and liturgist. Her position in the congregation is that of a traditional specialized ministry, but she also leads the mission of the congregation. She has particularly helped us to see the need in the public school system, where she is occasionally employed as a substitute teacher. The schools are woefully underfunded in a context where the people with financial resources send their children to private school. White flight has taken a huge toll on public schools. The congregation has developed a partnership with the middle school just down the road, and we look forward to more cooperative projects in the future that will increase the opportunities for students to succeed. Similar stories can be told about the work of deacons in many congregations. As the recent Study of Ministry report says, "deacons help the church love the world with the compassionate heart of Jesus and confront the powers of the world" (2020, 1013–1014).

Study of Ministry Report for General Conference 2020 Addresses Unresolved Issues

Unresolved issues remain in the ordering of ministry in The United Methodist Church. Yet again, in 2016, a Study of Ministry Commission, with its own budget and leadership, was established to take them on. This commission identified the most urgent inconsistency as the linkage of ordination and sacrament. Because the UMC continues to authorize laypersons (licensed local pastors) for sacramental presidency, it is breaking its own rules. And, of course, some of the UMC's ordained persons (deacons) are not usually authorized to offer the sacraments. In the spring of 1996, the Diaconal Clearness Committee agreed among themselves that they would surrender on this issue to get the ordained deacon approved, if it became necessary. And they did. In 1996, elders who objected to the idea of ordaining persons who would not be pastors of congregations felt that they should at least hang onto the privilege of offering sacraments. Reserving this ministry for elders gave them some sense of uniqueness or authority. And many of them were quick to explain that they had agreed to itinerate. They argued that, in giving up the right to choose where they would be appointed, they should hang onto something else—sacramental authority.

The question now is whether that disconnect between ordination and sacrament will continue. Fewer and fewer of our active elders have been ordained as probationary deacons; that practice ended in 1996. Many United Methodists have attended theological schools where student colleagues were preparing to be both elders and deacons and have come through that experience with deep appreciation for each other's call and identity. The complementarity is appreciated; the competition is lessening. Another twenty years will bring a new day of creative ministries for both elders and deacons.

The Study of Ministry that will be considered at the next General Conference[1] addresses this inconsistency and argues that both ordained orders should be authorized to preside at the eucharistic meal.

> When ordained elders and deacons lead the peoples' prayer together at the Table, they represent this dual movement of offering ourselves to God, who then offers us back to the world, the transformed ones who become agents of transformation. Together, the two orders appropriately and helpfully lead the people in the eucharistic movement of turning toward God in worship and turning toward the world in service" (2020, 1011).

The section on the Order of Deacons ends with this: "Our theological understanding creates space for deacons, by virtue of their ordination, to administer the sacraments" (1014). Unlike the current Disciplinary statements related to deacons and sacrament, this one is unequivocal. Deacon Amy Aspey attests to the appreciation of deacons that this commission expressed. "I was grateful for the opportunity to serve as a Ministry Study Commission member and experienced the team to be supportive and affirming to the order of Deacon and its essential role in the future of The United Methodist Church," she says.

Another unresolved issue relates to itineration. The Methodist tradition in the United States was that "traveling preachers" agreed to go wherever the bishop sent them each year. That willingness to itinerate was essential for full conference membership. Since 1996, some elders have been jealous of the seeming freedom deacons have to find a place that matches their calling and gifts. Of course, the bishop has the authority and responsibility of appointing each deacon, and the deacon must convince the bishop that this place of service will extend the mission of the church. These same elders often forget that, with freedom, comes the risk of no appointment at all and unemployment. With elders' agreement to itinerate comes a guaranteed appointment and often a parsonage in which to live. However, some in the church believe that we can no longer even afford to promise guaranteed appointments for elders. If that is the case, perhaps itinerating will also need to be reconsidered. The Study of Ministry report expresses it this way: "Elders are both sent out in mission through itineracy and lead the church in mission. Deacons identify the type and location of their ministries and are appointed to and lead missional ministries in both the church and world" (1016). Both deacons and elders are "sent out into mission" (1016). Economics may dictate new ways of deploying and supporting our ordained leaders.

The 2016–2020 Study of Ministry report includes a proposal for ordaining the laypeople who currently serve as licensed local pastors. They would be a new class called *local elders*. Ordination and sacrament could then be linked. Laity would no longer be licensed to preside at the sacraments. With the clarification that deacons too are linked to sacrament by their ordination, one inconsistency would be eliminated. "Through ordination, the Holy Spirit empowers, and the church authorizes" (1012). According to the current *Discipline*, both elders and deacons become full members of the annual conference with the right to vote on all matters, including clergy delegates to the General Conference and "responsibility for all matters of ordination, character, and conference relations of clergy" (2016, ¶329.2). Ordained deacons are full members of the conference; this was an acknowledgment that their missional leadership in the world equips them to shape the mission of the conference alongside elders.

The 2020 report proposes that non-itinerating clergy would be considered *local elders*. They would not participate in the ordering of the conference as full members. The caution I would raise to this proposal is that deacons do not itinerate in the same way that elders do, and this could open the door to designating deacons as *local* too. This effectively would take the voices that are attuned to the "petty fiefdoms of this world in which human will and desire still hold sway" (Study 2020, 1010) out of the decision-making that shapes the church at its highest levels. Members of the commission have reassured me that they did not intend that, but unintended consequences sometimes develop, and this would be a very significant step away from that value.

Whatever happens in regard to this Study of Ministry report, the fact remains that the UMC has deacons serving and leading who are particularly attuned to injustice. The range of locations for their ministry continues to expand. In each case, the church is there, participating in God's mission, and the deacon connects back to a congregation and invites it to join in the mission. The promise of the deacon is yet to be fully realized because there are so few, but in each place where a deacon is appointed, the Word is enfleshed.

The order is now established and has expanded the reach of the UMC as deacons have been appointed to schools, hospitals, nonprofits, and all sorts of other places for ministries of compassion and justice. Deacons are participating boldly in God's mission in the world. United Methodist laypersons are in all those places too, earnestly seeking to live out their call as baptized Christians. The baptismal covenant asks, "Do you accept the freedom and power God gives you to resist evil, injustice, and oppression in whatever forms they present themselves?" (*UMH* 1989, 40). When an ordained deacon is in those same places, the difference is that the deacon brings a calling, an ordained identity, theological sophistication, and accountability to the local church along with their skills for their work in the world. A deacon who is a special education teacher, for instance, has been certified for that work and knows a great deal about the variety of developmental issues that the children are facing and how to help them succeed. But that deacon also applies his theological training to appreciate the diversity and beauty of God's creation found in the classroom as motivation to advocate for justice for those children. Because the bishop has appointed the deacon to that place, the church has affirmed its desire to be there with compassion and justice.

What is a deacon? A deacon is an extension of the mission of the church, an extension of the eucharistic table of grace, wherever she or he is appointed. A deacon is also accountable to the UMC, accountable to uphold the highest standard of ethics to bring the needs of the world to the local church. Deacons are entrepreneurs, seeking out places to respond to the calling that God has placed on their hearts. Deacons are enfleshed representatives of Christ, seeking to contribute to the transformation of the world. Deacons are embodied mission.[2]

9 Already, but Not Yet

This book was written to celebrate the courageous and creative decision that was made in 1996. The reordering of ministry in The United Methodist Church created two distinct, complementary, and equal orders, each contributing to the mission of the church but from different vantage points. Indeed, the UMC was at the leading edge of Christianity with this conceptualization. In the UMC version, the permanent diaconate shares parity with the presbyter (elder) and is envisioned as central to the mission of the church. There is so much to celebrate in this vision of mutuality that enhances and stimulates mission. Paragraph 201 of the *Discipline* tells us that "the church exists for the maintenance of worship, the edification of believers, and the redemption of the world." Deacons and elders provide leadership for these tasks from distinct points of view and with distinct, complementary gifts. This seems like a recipe for vitality and fruitfulness. The vision for fulfilling the mission is already present.

Yet that vision of elder, deacon, and people of God sharing in ministry and mission is not yet fully present. This chapter will describe some of the barriers to full contribution of the order of deacon. One barrier is linked to the misunderstanding of *service* and how it has supported the second, sexism. A third barrier is racism and White privilege, which has not created a diverse diaconate that reflects the diverse people of God and the communities who are our neighbors. A fourth barrier to fulfilling the promise of the deacon is lack of financial and mission support for ministries with poor and marginalized people.

Barrier #1: Misunderstanding of Service

The name of this office, *deacon*, is part of the first barrier to its full realization. In recent memory for United Methodists, the word *deacon* denoted someone who was on probation, the transitional deacon. The deacon was a first stage of ordination and under supervision by an elder. "When are you going to be a real minister?" springs from that old understanding. It has been twenty-five years since 1996; that kind of *deacon* is no longer being ordained, but the notion that a deacon is not yet fully approved still affects deacons.

Other denominations also use the term deacon and in most cases it denotes a lay person who is a leader in a congregation. In a culture where people often choose a congregation for its activities or its preacher and are often changing from one denomination to another, the profusion of meanings for the word *deacon* can leave most people unaware of the particular meaning of the United Methodist deacon. Our congregations are full of former Baptists or Presbyterians whose experience of deacons is different.

In addition, the root of the word *deacon* is the Greek term *diakonia*. In most English translations of the Bible, it has been rendered as *servant* or *service*. The term occurs repeatedly in the New Testament. If one is not on guard, the deacon, by association, becomes thought of like a servant or slave. However, we must remember that, when Greek-speaking people used the term *diakonia* in the first century it also meant go-between or messenger. This understanding is very fitting for an office that is described as connecting world and church. Deacons are intermediaries who move between the church and the needs of the world as God leads them, but few United Methodists are aware of this clarification.

Serving others is a way to be a good neighbor. There is nothing wrong with serving, but the critical question is, serving who? If we keep in mind that all who are ordained are serving God, then it is very appropriate. In practice, it has been too easy for deacons to be seen as the servant of the elder in charge. When the majority of deacons are women, that trap is wide open, and many have fallen into it due to the influence of residual patriarchal values! The *Discipline* has explicitly addressed this trap with ¶131: "There is but one ministry in Christ, but there are diverse gifts and evidences of God's grace in the body of Christ. . . . No ministry is subservient to another." And service is also explicitly named in the ordination for elders to Word, service, sacrament, and order. Yet, sometimes, the old assumptions hang on from the time when an ordained deacon was a transitional place where one was proving oneself qualified to be ordained as an elder.

Deacons are also sometimes their own worst enemies. Charles R. Foster sounded the alarm about this in *Quarterly Review* when he wrote, "When diaconal ministers direct their attention to congregational life rather than to the way congregational life embodies the servanthood of Jesus Christ in the world, then the diaconate can only contribute to the domestication of the church's mission." Christian educators have been especially prone to this. When they count success as more and more participants in events with more and more fancy themes and decorations, they have lost track of the true goal of making disciples who seek to transform the world. Foster encouraged diaconal ministers to stay focused on the mission with "careful, sustained, and systematic theological reflection on the nature of the church and its mission" (Spring 1991, 33).

What Foster wrote in 1991 is equally true today. Deacons must keep their eyes focused on cooperating with God in the redemption of the world, eliminating White privilege, and bringing the kin-dom[1] of God to fruition. This focus is especially important when elders are pressured to produce ever higher attendance and more dollars rather than offering prophetic ministry that addresses injustice. Deacons and elders under this pressure need to be colleagues who encourage one another's creativity and prophetic ministry. No ministry is subservient to another, and all must keep their eye on the greater mission. The work of deacons must be in service to the mission of the church, God's vision of peace and justice.

Because the COVID-19 pandemic shut buildings and *church* is happening in new ways, perhaps the work of elders can be refocused too. Many are asking for a reexamination of the meaning of *church*. The buildings are not at the heart of the church. The worship of God, relationships of the people, and their missional work in the world is at the heart. As the church is reconsidered, perhaps it is time for a reconsideration of the orders of ministry. What does the elder do? What does the deacon do? We may be in a place where creative reconsideration of how we order our ministry should happen to respond to this new situation.

Foster noted that a theological consideration of power could be especially critical for the diaconate:

> When one enters into the service of another one takes on inferior or marginal or liminal status. The child, the stranger, the person who is different, the servant all relate to social organizations on the margins, in places of inferiority or as residents of two worlds or communities. They do not possess traditional institutional forms of power. But they do have power (1991, 34).

What is that power? Foster's example is a crying baby among adults. Everyone in the room is aware of the unhappiness of the child. This small, powerless human has power! But is that the kind of power deacons seek? Do deacons need to cry out with shrill sounds? I think not. Yet sometimes they have taken that approach as they sought pensions, political power, or secure employment. These are important justice issues for deacons, but myopic vision can leave the diaconate focused on these and lose the commitment to the mission that should remain foremost.

When deacons have spoken out of their passion for justice and relationship with the marginalized, they have changed minds and impacted the mission of the church. The truths they know about the needs of the world and their own faithful lives have caused the church to listen and act. One example is the deacon who worked with a labor union for hotel workers. He taught us about the workers who cleaned rooms, lifted heavy mattresses to make the beds, dealt with messes created by guests, but lacked health-insurance support or paid time off when they were sick or injured. Many in his conference have never forgotten about those workers and always leave a generous tip in the room for them.

Another example comes from an educator whose ministry of leading a group called Reading Women opened some eyes and hearts to the marginalized through liberation theology and biblical study that included a wide range of hermeneutical points of view. One privileged, White woman shaped by that reading wrote, "Yesterday we cried together, black and white children of God cried together. The white participants recognized the pain of our black brothers and sisters and the fear they carry all of the time." She attributes her commitment to the Black Lives Matter movement to her participation in Reading Women nearly thirty years ago. For a White person of her cultural and social status, this is quite remarkable. Teaching that focuses on the ultimate transformation of the world as its theological guide can change attitudes and make a difference. A deacon has power through the questions asked in a Bible study and leading discussion that dares to experiment with new ideas. There is power even from the liminal space in the hierarchy that servanthood would seem to imply.

Barrier #2: Unconscious Sexism Limits Deacons

Sustaining this notion that deacons are servants is the fact that so many deacons are women. (I estimate that about 80 percent of deacons are women, but statistics are difficult to obtain.) Despite the great progress that women have made and the many professions that have opened to women, patriarchal values and assumptions are still very much a part of US culture and The United Methodist Church. Even at the level of a general agency, implicit sexism was present. Rosalie Bentzinger joined the GBHEM staff and headed the Division of Diaconal Ministry, which should have been at the same level as the Division of Ordained Ministry. But Joaquin Garcia recalls: "For many years, Rosalie was the only female associate general secretary in the Secretarial Council. She often would offer ideas or recommendations, and no one would say anything! Then, when one of the "guys" said *exactly* the same thing, they paid attention and responded! Rosalie and I used to joke that she needed to learn to play tennis or golf in order to be "one of the guys." As they were playing, they came to consensus about an idea, recommendation, or project, and then discussed it in order to get agreement from the Secretarial Council."

When a deacon joins the staff of a congregation, more likely than not the senior pastor is male. Sometimes the deacon is seen as an ordained professional colleague. Sometimes, unfortunately, the deacon is seen primarily as the senior pastor's employee or assistant. This happens too often when the senior pastor is male, and the deacon is female. Some senior pastors are encouraged to behave as if other clergy on the staff are just contract employees. This attitude ignores the fact that those clergy, both elders and deacons, are appointed by the bishop. The bishop and cabinet discerned that this deacon or elder has gifts that can advance the mission of the church in that context. Deacons bring a specialized ministry to the congregation and are not in competition with the elder in charge. Consciously or unconsciously, the sexist values of the surrounding culture seep into the church. Too many instances of elders who have not honored the calling or gifts of a deacon mar the history of the interaction of orders that are complementary, distinct, and equal.

As the new order of deacon was being established, it seemed that it had the potential to overcome the sexism that infected many diaconal ministers' situations. Jack Harnish realized in 1996 that helping the denomination live into the new order would not be easy. He saw that diaconal ministers who transitioned into ordained ministry would need a new sense of their identity and their place in the conference. Boards of Ordained Ministry would need to reorganize for their larger agenda. The mission of the church at the time, "to spread scriptural holiness and reform the continent" had not changed, however, and he knew that the two ordained offices offered "new tools" for the work. Harnish and Jimmy Carr formed a partnership to get it done.

Sexist attitudes were lying in wait, however. Lynn Scott, a colleague who was also on the staff of GBHEM at that time, voiced a concern that many shared. She knew that research had revealed that women comprised just 13 percent of United Methodist clergy in 1996, when the term *clergy* applied only to elders. The diaconal ministers were just the opposite; 75 percent of diaconal ministers were women. Scott told *The Flyer*, COSROW's newsletter,

> What we do know is that women leave church ministry at a higher rate than men. Women leave ministry for lots of reasons, but they define their ordained, sacramental ministry in a broader perspective than men tend to. When we consider this information in light of the sexism, gender discrimination, and power factors that women deal with every day, we have to wonder whether there will be a subtle or unconscious tracking of women into deacon's orders. (Summer/Fall 1996, 3)

Reading Scott's comment twenty-five years later leaves one breathless at its prescience. After all this time, it is still true that women leave church ministry at a higher rate than men. In Northern Illinois, those of us on the Board of Ordained Ministry were shocked by the numbers of clergywomen on disability leave compared to men! Stress takes a toll on the bodies of women in ministry with their complex family responsibilities and the sexist resistance that is always present.

It is also still true that men are often discouraged from pursuing deacon's orders. As a faculty member of a United Methodist seminary, I heard many stories of young male students who had discerned a call to the diaconate who were pushed hard by their District Committee on Ministry and the

Conference Board to be an elder instead. Much of that pressure was not subtle, although the sexism at the root of it may have been subconscious. Most of us are so shaped by traditional patriarchal values that we unconsciously see more potential for leadership in men and the image of pastor prevails. *The Flyer* reported in August 2014 that many people were still being discouraged from being deacons: "men because the order of elder begets prestige and authority, and women because people believe they should aspire to what men want, to reach the *top*" (1). The writer restated the ongoing problem:

> Elders function in a "head of the household" type of role in that they administer sacraments and keep order. Deacons are viewed more as helpers or servants. Living in a culture where the overarching expectations place men in authoritative, administrative roles makes it difficult for people to picture men as being adequately fulfilled in a role that is defined by exclusion from headship.

The article also discussed the devaluing of feminized labor such as social work, nursing, and teaching and cited a study that showed that deacons have an 18 percent lower salary than elders with other indicators being equal. Ordained deacons struggle to find equality with these realities staring them in the face. Yet, many answer the call to be deacons and to lead the church in its mission from that order.

One other aspect of sexism that needs to be named here comes from ecumenical documents, particularly *Baptism, Eucharist, Ministry.* Although this document cites Galatians 3:28—that in Christ there is neither male nor female—it does not take a clear stand on the ordination of women. In fact, after acknowledging that some churches believe that only men are eligible for ordination, it states, "Differences on these issues raise obstacles to the mutual recognition of ministries. But those obstacles must not be regarded as substantive hindrance for further efforts toward mutual recognition" (1982, 32). The ecumenical community chose not to confront sexism in the church. The sexist tradition had pushed women who were called to ministry into the deaconess movement, the one place open to them since the mid-nineteenth century. Deaconesses do very important ministry. Unfortunately, they remain at the missional margins of the church, supported primarily by women's groups and basically cloistered.

Ordination with full clergy rights was not open to women in The United Methodist Church until 1956, with the first woman elder elected bishop only in 1980. Women struggled for full participation in the church for many years. And then along came the deacon, which is primarily women, many of whom are specialists in the kinds of work with which women have much experience such as teaching, social work, caring for the sick, and feeding hungry people. Of course, sexism dogged it from the beginning!

Barrier #3: Lack of Awareness of Systemic Racism

The persistence of sexism is not the only barrier to the full realization of the deacon. Systemic racism is present too. Along with its heavy population of women, the order of deacon has remained very White. Deacons serve a denomination that remains overwhelmingly White in the United States. And White culture has been blind to its systemic racism. The UMC story of inclusion is a mixed one. For years, the existence of the Central Jurisdiction institutionalized segregation and lagged behind US public efforts to integrate. However, the church does seek to address systemic racism. The work of the General Board of Church and Society is helping to teach us about the ways we, perhaps unwittingly, have perpetuated White privilege and how we might address more just ways of being the church. The ordination of deacons takes place within this mixed story. The Council of Bishops named Dismantling Racism a major initiative for the denomination in 2020.

Joaquin Garcia was interviewed in Fall of 1981 for GBHEM's newsletter, *Colleague*. The writer, Charles Cole from the GBHEM Office of Interpretation wrote, "Joaquin also reported a new interest in diaconal ministry by ethnic persons, probably due in part to the thirteen ethnic minority projects currently supported by the division." Bentzinger and Garcia, with the support of the board directors, were working hard to address the lack of diversity among diaconal ministers. Hiring Garcia in 1979, a native of Mexico who was a graduate of Scarritt College's Christian Education program in Nashville, Tennessee, was a critically important decision in support of broadening the makeup of diaconal ministry, in both gender and ethnicity. Garcia has never lost his commitment to increasing diversity in the diaconate. The Convocation of 2003 was evidence of that value with its many representatives from the global diaconate. And as we confront the legacy of racism and White privilege in the United States, the need to raise up voices from the margins of culture has never been more important. However, no ethnic minority projects are currently addressed to deacons.

In 1989, Paul Van Buren and Daniel Lee, a diaconal minister and professor of social work, undertook a qualitative research study sponsored by the Division of Diaconal Ministry of GBHEM. They interviewed many people who were associated with ethnic minority congregations in the UMC in the United States. Their purpose was "to assist The United Methodist Church and the Division of Diaconal Ministry to be more responsive to meeting the needs of ethnic minority churches and communities through persons in diaconal forms of ministry" (Lee and Van Buren, 10). They found that the term *diaconal minister* had "very limited acceptance and usage among certain ethnic groups" (71). They also found that many ethnic minority churches expressed needs that diaconal ministers were equipped to offer. The congregations needed youth ministers, social workers, Christian educators, community organizers, and experts in day care for children (71–73). The mismatch between acceptance of diaconal ministry and needs was clear. This is a clear mandate for the future.

Some ethnic minority candidates report that their own community scoffs at a call to deacon, claiming that he or she should choose the greater power of the elder. And ethnic minority women face the competing pressures: choose elder for greater prestige and power; choose deacon because they are women. All of this is based on the flawed notion that the elder is higher in the hierarchy than the deacon. Concerted efforts to identify ethnic minority candidates for deacon and to support them financially could begin to address many of those yearnings for leaders with specialized ministry skills that were identified in that study. Those needs are still there. Why can't we identify, train, and appoint deacons who are called and equipped to address them!

Barrier #4: Lack of Financial Support for Missional Ministries with Marginalized People

In late 1995, as diaconal ministers were organizing for the push toward the 1996 General Conference, Barbara Garcia wrote to the diaconal ministers in the Tennessee Conference that the question they must keep uppermost was, "In what ways does the structure of the new permanent ordained deacon enhance mission and ministry with the poor and marginalized, which is a priority in our conference?" The 1996 legislation created an order that was conceived as complementary, distinct, and equal to the order of elder. What it did not ensure was that there would be funding to support deacons as they responded to the opportunities for ministry with the poor and marginalized. Instead, congregations with large membership were almost the only sources of employment. Conferences have been slow to support ministries where deacons could actually address the injustices of poverty, racism, and sexism. Some deacons have succeeded in finding places to serve with nonprofits that address those goals. But while many persons have heard a call to the work, too many have not been able to find a way to support it. The UMC needs to be identifying, recruiting, encouraging, training, ordaining, and supporting people who match communities of need—linguistically and culturally—to go to those places and bring the sacramental presence of the church. In addition, deacons should be sent to the crossroads of power in cities and states where they can advocate for justice. The mission of the UMC needs people of all races, gender identities, ethnicities, and language groups who are called by God and are willing to go to these places of need where injustice flourishes.

Already, but Not Yet

A piece of this picture that greatly complicates the situation is that the specialized GBHEM staff position leading the work of deacons, which had offered critically important leadership and support for the order since 1972, no longer exists. After the retirement of Joaquin Garcia in 2003, the GBHEM restructured and combined the three Ministry Sections. Anita D. Wood and Sharon Rubey carried the work of resourcing the order of deacons forward with added responsibilities. They met with seminaries, trained Boards of Ordained Ministry and district superintendents, led formation events for provisional deacons, helped to sponsor convocations, and lifted up the ecumenical *diakonia* through DOTAC and World Diakonia. When Wood retired in 2013, Victoria Rebeck became the director of Deacon Ministry Development and Provisional Membership Support. She advocated for the order of deacon as well as helping boards to maintain standards and processes. In 2018, her position was eliminated.

Another deacon, Meg Lassiat, joined the GBHEM staff in 2005 as director of Enlistment and Recruitment. Lassiat worked cross divisionally, serving in both the Division of Higher Education and the Division of Ministry. She was the first deacon who joined the GBHEM staff in a position that was not specifically related to deacon. Dr. Kathy Armistead, a deacon, became editor for Wesley's Foundery Books, a highly regarded academic press published by

GBHEM.[2] Her work was not specifically related to deacons, but she served the whole church by publishing many significant books. Unfortunately, as of the writing of this book, both Lassiat and Armistead have left and no deacon is part of the full-time GBHEM staff.

In response to the changing realities and needs of the church, GBHEM has identified new ways to engage its work with the ministry of the deacon. GBHEM will continue to identify a staff person who serves as the primary liaison with the Order of Deacons but has extended its understanding of deacon support as an agency-wide priority. GBHEM understands that it is the work of all staff to consider how deacons impact, and are impacted by, all of their work. Key to broadening deacon support has been the development of a deacon's advisory and advocacy council that, in collaborative partnership with GBHEM staff, identifies and responds to the needs and concerns of deacons.

Especially good news for deacons is that the leadership of GBHEM is no longer questioning the existence of the order of deacon. General Secretary Greg Bergquist offers this statement of support:

> The ordained Deacon is called by God and set apart by the church for the ministry of Word, Service, Compassion and Justice, leading the church into the public square as the people called United Methodist articulate, embrace, and embody our servant ministry in a world longing for transformation. I believe that the order of Deacons is uniquely positioned to provide the kind of faithful and innovative leadership required as The United Methodist Church envisions and reimagines the mission and ministry of the church into the future. GBHEM is honored to be in collaborative partnership with ordained Deacons throughout the connection as we embrace our new reality, and the adaptive opportunities God has set before us.

This chapter's title, *Already, but Not Yet* is a phrase used by theologians to refer to the idea that the kin-dom of God is already here but not fully realized. In Matthew's Gospel, Jesus says, "Proclaim the good news, The kingdom of heaven has come near. Cure the sick, raise the dead, cleanse the lepers, cast out demons" (Matthew 10:7-8 NRSV). And in Luke 6:20 (NRSV): "Blessed are you who are poor, / for yours is the kingdom of God." The kin-dom is already here, but not fully realized. The promise of the order of deacons is also already here. The way it was conceptualized and the way many deacons are living into it is already enfleshing its promise. Ordained deacons are fighting for justice in many places. Ordained deacons are teaching the UMC about its ingrained sexism and White privilege with its resultant systemic racism and sexism. Deacons are forming young Christians who have served Christ by loving their neighbors. Deacons have been leaders in the efforts to help the denomination abandon its homophobia. Deacons regularly remind their annual conferences about marginalized people who should be heard and supported. Deacons proclaim that Black Lives Matter. The list could go on and on of the ways that deacons are already proclaiming and embodying the Word as they serve God with ministries of compassion and justice. But the potential is not yet realized for this great vision.

10 A Vision for the Future

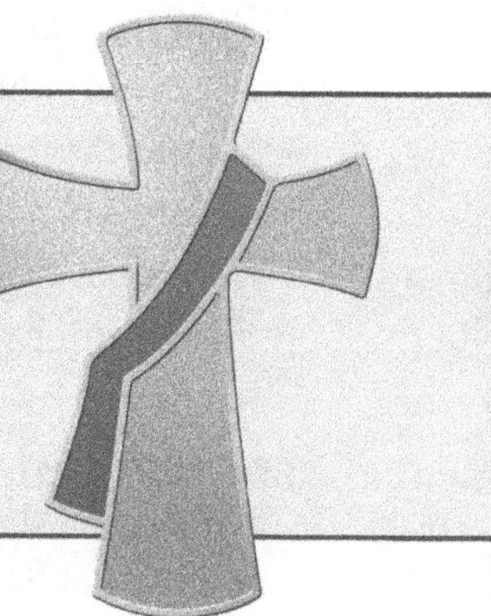

Over the centuries, times of turmoil have brought about a renewal of the diaconate. This book has been written in a time of enormous turmoil; crisis is on every hand. The twin pandemics of the COVID-19 virus and systemic racism threaten our health. In response to the COVID-19 virus, we were asked to stay home and avoid contact with other people. Because we stayed home, many businesses have been forced to close, which has brought economic stress to our communities. People whose jobs were in offices have been able to work from home, but many others risk infection from the virus when they go to their jobs, or they have already lost their jobs due to the shutdown. Many schools are closed too, and children are supposed to learn virtually from home. Suddenly, parents have had to become teachers. Even schools that have opened for in-person learning are operating very differently.

Through the impact of the COVID-19 pandemic, the pandemic of systemic racism in the United States has been revealed as never before. The eight minutes and forty-six seconds that the Minneapolis policeman's knee was on George Floyd's neck have awakened and reawakened many Americans to the reality of injustices fed by systemic racism. The Black Lives Matter movement is energized and will not rest until change has been wrought. Diverse groups of young people have led the way in many cities. People of faith are reenergized to stand for inclusion for all.

Everything is under scrutiny. And we experienced a conflicted and challenged presidential election. Some Americans believe that the election results were fraudulent. Insurrectionists threatened our national capitol and the leaders who were working there. The turmoil and division are almost overwhelming in the United States. But this turmoil is also global. The virus threatens people everywhere, and the economic fallout is present on every continent. Climate change threatens the health of the planet itself, disproportionately affecting vulnerable populations. The scope of the turmoil is unprecedented. What is happening to the order of deacon in these times of turmoil?

Unfortunately, in addition to the cultural turmoil, there is turmoil in The United Methodist Church. The United Methodist Church has come to an impasse in its debate about human sexuality. There is a very real possibility that some division or divisions will occur at the next General Conference. As this book is written, the postponed General Conference of 2020 looms large, yet it seems far off. It may be virtual, or it may not ever convene. We are fighting a global pandemic with no idea when it might relent and let us travel or see one another face-to-face again. Because of the pandemic, most church buildings were closed, and the activity of the congregation happened in new ways. Perhaps the turmoil is simply too much, and the diaconate will not have an opportunity to respond. Perhaps the church will contract and withdraw behind its walls.

When diaconal ministry was proposed in 1976, Rena Yocom's voice was persuasive and prophetic. She sought ecclesiastical validation of her call to ministry. Her understanding of the diaconate comes from the perspective of ecumenical Christianity. As she looks down the long view of Christianity over the centuries, she sees that "rapid political and economic change" often spur more reliance on the diaconate "when the sacramental ministry at the altar is not sufficient to express our faith and love of God." How is the deacon one answer for the church in today's turmoil?

Deacons Are One Answer for These Tumultuous Times

United Methodists are not ready to give up on the church's mission. No! The church congregation has left the building, but it is still the church. "The church is not a building. The church is not a steeple. The church is not a resting place. The church is a people" (*UMH*, 558). The words of this little song by Avery and Marsh were way ahead of their time. And the people have a mission in the world: God's mission of hope, reconciliation, justice, healing, new life, and life-giving community. Yes. Perhaps most buildings will be repurposed.

We are experiencing the church as people connected by technologies, but we are still in mission. The skills in theological reflection of deacons, elders, and faithful laity have kept the church on track. People of faith have sought the direction and call of God in these tumultuous times. Congregations have found needs in their communities and have responded. Food has been distributed to children and families. Pastoral care has been offered through phone calls, virtual visits, parades of cars, and waving from a distance. More people participate in online worship services than came to services in person. Small groups for learning abound and meet via Zoom or other online platforms. Giving continues. The church is a people who have been resourceful and creative in this pandemic time. Church people have stood in solidarity and led in ministries of justice and inclusion, calling for new ways to interact with one another. The denomination has resourced this justice work with webinars and curriculum for study groups. The term *antiracist* has been added to our vocabularies, and many White methodists are hoping to learn how to be antiracists.

Frankly and more important, the Black Lives Matter movement has shown the church that it is not immune. It too has systemic racism at its heart, which must be lamented, exposed, and eradicated.

Who better to lead this than deacons who are ordained to Word, service, compassion, and justice?

If the church is a people, then what kind of leadership do the people called United Methodist need for this next era? This is one of those moments of turmoil when something new might be born. Almost overnight, the leaders of congregations, lay and clergy, had to learn how to create worship that could be offered virtually. They rose to the challenge, and many congregations are discovering that more and different people are connecting with their worship online and throughout the week. What a surprise! Clearly, we need leaders—ordained and lay—with skills in technology when face-to-face meetings are not safe. Sunday school classes, some quite elderly, have figured out how to use Zoom and still gather weekly to learn and share their prayer concerns and talk about how to be disciples in this difficult time. All of that is keeping the church going. But is that enough?

An online seminar offered by GBHEM, "Leading in Crisis" (August 12, 2020), featured several leaders, including Dr. F. Douglas Powe Jr.[1] Powe offered a set of categories that emphasized that churches grow through community engagement. His presentation offered illustrations of different kinds of churches and their mission in our world. What he termed the *swamp* churches are standing still and decaying. The *reservoir* churches have some resources but are mostly doing things *for* people. This is the *care* model of leadership. *Canal* congregations make connections with the world and partner with people. I was struck by this last category because it is exactly what the deacon is ordained to lead, to connect world and church, serving as a bridge or conduit, like a canal connects two places by water. These are helpful categories. However, the deacon was never mentioned in the seminar. The underlying assumption was that the elder was the only leader available to aid in becoming a canal congregation. That is not true. Many laypersons are ready and able to lead this mission. Deacons are ordained to lead in this work. That is the definition of the deacon: to connect the church with the needs of the world. I long for the day when leaders of the church will think, *how can our deacons help us?* Elders are not the only leaders for the church. The complementary ministry of the deacon and the embodied ministry of the laity will join in partnership to follow God into the world.

Deacon Victoria Rebeck, the last person to be employed by GBHEM explicitly to support deacons, writes:

> Among the adaptive questions that the denomination could be asking are (1) Do we believe that it is pastors who provide ministry and everyone else receives it? Have we taken the ministry of the laity away from them? Could that be contributing to the weakness of our denomination? and (2) How important is compassion and justice to Christian discipleship? Is the world hungry for those expressions of Christian faith? If we believe that love of God and love of neighbor are the summary of all God's law, would we not want an order of clergy who take lifelong vows to lead the church in these areas?

We have this order of clergy!

In 1999, Kenneth E. Rowe, then the Methodist librarian and professor of Church History at Drew University, wrote an article about the deacon for *Quarterly Review.* He was writing shortly after the 1996 decision. He said, "It is absolutely crucial to take into our hearts and into our polity a diaconate primarily concerned with dreaming dreams of a humane world and leading the rest of us to find a place to minister to Christ in the person of the needy." Having summarized the history of the diaconate, he also wrote, "It is too scriptural an office, too closely related to the heart of Christianity, to be left entirely to chance—especially for people called Methodists" (355). Coming from a professor of church history, those were powerful words in 1999. They are still powerful words now.

What Do Deacons Need?

In 1996, The United Methodist Church dreamed of deacons who would lead the church in its mission to the world and address injustice wherever it is found. We have that deacon. The order is well established, and the standards are high. We have fresh and urgent information about the injustices of the world. Let's run with it!

The sticking points remain. They are itineracy, sacrament, and economics. The 2020 Study of Ministry report asks the church to consider ordination. Inevitably, the discussion will include those sticking points. Deacons do not itinerate in the same way that elders do. Deacons will need to help the church see that they itinerate in response to God's call and the bishop's confirmation.

This Study of Ministry also affirms that deacons, by virtue of their ordination, should be offering the sacraments in their ministry. The Study seems focused on the need to have ordained leadership for the congregation's sacramental life. Perhaps we need more sustained theological discussions about where the mediating grace of Holy Communion needs to be offered. Where are the people who would be sustained by regular participation in the sacrament? How can we go to them? As John Wesley dared to go out to preach in fields, perhaps we must dare to go to the places where people without housing are encamped and offer the mediating grace of God through Holy Communion. We need more sustained theological reflection about how God calls the faithful into ministries in the world. Where is God acting now in the world? How can we cooperate with God's mission? Who can go there? Deacons?

The UMC has never taken economic responsibility for its Order of Deacons. A deacon who cannot support himself or herself is simply abandoned. Perhaps, in a new, post–COVID-19 world, the idea of circuits will surface once again. I can imagine a circuit with several small congregations with both a deacon and an elder appointed there. The deacon would equip the laity for intervening in the places where vulnerable people need support, whether for food or better schools or to stop unjust policing practices. In many of the circuits, several parsonages may be rented out or sitting empty because the congregation cannot afford a full-time elder. A deacon could live there, participate in the community, build a mission powered by laity, and contribute to the kin-dom of God.

To thrive, The United Methodist Church needs the complementarity of elders, deacons, and laity. Each has a particular focus, and each can contribute to the task of discerning God's will and then implementing it. Deacons bring theological training to their work in both church and world. Their commitment to "engage the world with a heart of compassion and a prophetic longing for God's justice to prevail" (Study 2020, 1013) can help the church keep moving toward the kin–dom. Elders are essential to the health and functioning of a congregation; they are ordained to order the church. Laity are the church. Together, they make a great team.

We need attention and help from the whole church to think about, support, and encourage deacons who are called to lead people from our congregations into their discipleship in the world. Chapter after chapter in this book has attested to the leadership from the General Board of Higher Education and Ministry that helped to keep the order of deacons on track and theologically sound. Over and over, the staff of the Division of Deacons provided gatherings where deacons (and before that, diaconal ministers) could find rest, renewal, and energy for their ministry. Deacon Adrienne Ann Ilsemann describes the goal of the 2007 Convocation as creating "an oasis to step apart and to come together with others who shared our passion. Many of us weren't getting affirmation of our call and identity. It was so sweet" to be in a space cultivated by deacons for deacons. None of that is happening now because there is no staff and little funding to support deacons. It is lonely being a deacon. We need one another. In addition, there is no support from the general level of the church for deacon candidates. No formation events are being offered to help provisional deacons prepare for ordination. Their ordination does not fit the stereotype of the pastor. They must justify their call, teach the Board of Ordained Ministry about deacons, and survive the intense theological questioning. Nothing about the path is easy. Conferences need to step up.

Deacons Will Advocate for Their Ministry

The call to ordination as a deacon initiates in the individual; the Holy Spirit stirs up the heart and calls a person to focus their energy on compassion and justice in ways that are faithful to the Word. Then the arduous candidacy process proceeds for several years. As Linda Vogel wrote in 1991, "I became convinced that this was an invitation from my church to enter into a relationship of mutual responsibility and accountability as it claimed and affirmed the ministry God was calling me to do" ("Two Responses," 37). Deacon Nancy Lynne Westfield once said that the order of deacon was the church catching up to her call. Virginia Lee said that her call to ministry never changed. What changed in 1996 was how the church understood and named that call. Diaconal ministers worked for twenty years to convince the General Conference to fully affirm their call with ecclesiastical affirmation of that call. It happened in 1996. The 2022 General Conference will bring the huge institution that has been the UMC to a new place. As it divides, it will be smaller. Perhaps each of the smaller pieces will be more nimble. Perhaps the potential of the deacon will be set loose and supported. Deacons themselves will need to grab hold of things and convince the church to entrust them with the tasks at hand.

Deacons are taking matters into their own hands in many ways during the turmoil and crisis of the moment. They are leading marches for Black Lives Matter. They are writing books like Rebekah Jordan Gienapp's book on raising antiracist children. They are training lay volunteers to take a stand in the community. Adrienne Stricker affirms that she is hopeful about the ministries of deacons: "I find hope in the Order of Deacon every time I hear about a need for justice, and I can think of several deacons who have already been working in those areas." Stricker is co-chair of the order in her conference and in a position to know what deacons are doing. They are leading in compassion and justice.

We Have a Dream

The groundwork was there, but it really started with the hiring of Rosalie Bentzinger. As Joaquin Garcia says so eloquently,

> It was Rosalie who led the way with theologically sound, steady, high standards for the church to recognize the call of the people to a specific ministry connecting the church and the needs of the world in the very Wesleyan tradition. However, just like Moses leading the people in the desert to the promised land, the 1992 General Conference was Mount Nebo when God took Moses to see the promised land. In 1992 we got so close to establishing the Order of Deacon, but not yet there. Rosalie arrived to the 1992 General Conference and was able to see a glimpse of the Order of Deacon for The United Methodist Church, patterned on the early deacons' ministry. And with grace, faith, and hope, decided to retire and pass the torch to the next generation.

Just four years later, in 1996, it happened.

Rena Yocom's doctoral project about *diakonia*, written in 1991, ended with a paraphrase of Martin Luther King Jr.'s *I Have a Dream* speech. I reproduce it here because it is so timely. With the work King began very much before us now, and with John Lewis's recent death reminding us of all that nonviolent demonstrations stood for and the power for change of the civil rights movement, the 1963 March on Washington is much on my mind. Yocom's dream is my dream too.

> I have a dream that someday, someone will announce that they want to become a deacon . . . and the whole church will cheer and celebrate.
>
> I have a dream that someday people won't have to ask—what's a deacon? How come you're not a real minister? Could you be if you wanted to?
>
> I dream of a day when we won't need "deacon-under-glass." We won't have to be inspected or dissected or suspected. It will be a day when *deacon* doesn't need an adjective.
>
> I dream of a time when there is no ranking of ministries or ministers; no ranking of gender or race; only the belief that we are one in Christ Jesus.
>
> I dream of a time when the basin and towel speak as boldly about ministry as does the chalice.
>
> I dream of a day when deacons can be seen as care givers, demonstrating love and concern for all and calling the church into active involvement with the hurts and needs of humanity.
>
> I dream of a time when deacons are expected to be advocates, proclaiming justice, assisting the poor, the needy, and challenging the church to change systems which oppress.
>
> I dream of a time when deacons witness to the power of the Spirit as teachers and evangelists, inviting people to become disciples, nurturing them in faith.
>
> I dream of a day when deacons, lifting the global dimensions of the Christian faith, model the link between those gathered for worship and those scattered in the world.
>
> I dream of a time when the deacon so embodies servanthood that the people remember their call from the servant Christ.
>
> —Yocom 1991, 132–133

References

Advanced Daily Christian Advocate (ADCA). 1996; 2020. The United Methodist Publishing House.

Barnett, James Monroe. 1995. *The Diaconate: A Full and Equal Order*. Harrisburg, PA: Trinity Press International.

Bentzinger, Rosalie. 1991. *Putting an End to the Confusion: A Renewed Order of Deacon*. Occasional Papers No. 87. Nashville: General Board of Higher Education and Ministry.

The Book of Discipline of the United Methodist Church. 1976, 1980, 1984, 1988, 1992, 1996, 2000, 2004, 2008, 2012, 2016. Nashville: The United Methodist Publishing House.

Collins, John N. 1990. *Diakonia: Reinterpreting the Ancient Sources*. New York: Oxford University Press.

Conklin, Faith J. "To Serve the Present Age: Reflections on the Ministry Study Report." *Quarterly Review* 8 (1): 31–42.

Consultation on Church Union. 1985, Gerald F. Moede, ed. *The COCU Consensus: In Quest of a Church of Christ Uniting*. Princeton, NJ: Consultation on Church Union.

Crain, Margaret Ann, and Jack L. Seymour. 2001. *A Deacon's Heart: The New United Methodist Diaconate*. Nashville: Abingdon Press.

Crain, Margaret Ann, and Jack L. Seymour. 2003. *Yearning for God: Reflections of Faithful Lives*. Nashville: Upper Room Books.

Crain, Margaret Ann, 2007. *The Promise of the United Methodist Order of Deacon in the Twenty-First Century: Partners with the Whole People of God*. Nashville: General Board of Higher Education and Ministry.

Crain, Margaret Ann. 2014. *The United Methodist Deacon: Ordained to Word, Service, Compassion and Justice.* Nashville: Abingdon Press.

Daily Christian Advocate (DCA). 1980, 1984, 1988, 1992, 1996. Nashville: The United Methodist Publishing House.

The Discipline of the Evangelical United Brethren Church 1967. Dayton, Ohio: Board of Publication of the Evangelical United Brethren Church.

Foster, Charles R. 1991. "Diaconal Ministry: Vision and Reality." *Quarterly Review* 2 (1): 22–42.

Furnish, Dorothy Jean. 1976. *DRE/DCE—The History of a Profession.* Nashville: Christian Educators Fellowship of The United Methodist Church.

General Board of Higher Education and Ministry. *Colleague,* a newsletter. Fall 1981; Summer/Fall 1996; Winter/Spring 1999; Summer/Fall 2002; Summer/Fall 2003.

General Board of Higher Education and Ministry. *Yearbook.* 1974, 1976, 1994.

General Commission on the Status and Role of Women. *Women By the Numbers.* Published bi-monthly February 2005–January 2019. gcsrw.org.

General Commission on the Status and Role of Women. *The Flyer.* Summer/Fall 1996.

Gienapp, Rebekah. 2019. *Raising Antiracist Kids: An Age by Age Guide for Parents of White Children.* ebook @ www.thebarefootmommy.com

Handbook for Conference Board of Diaconal Ministry. 1992. Nashville: Division of Diaconal Ministry, General Board of Higher Education and Ministry.

Harnish, John E. 2000. *The Orders of Ministry in The United Methodist Church.* Nashville: Abingdon Press.

Hartley, Ben L. and Paul E. Van Buren. 2000. *The Deacon: Ministry Through Words of Faith and Acts of Love.* Nashville: Section of Deacons and Diaconal Ministries, General Board of Higher Education and Ministry.

Heitzenrater, Richard P. 1988. *A Critical Analysis of the Ministry Studies Since 1944.* Occasional Papers No. 76. Nashville: General Board of Higher Education and Ministry.

Johnson, Ethel R., Oral History. June 3, 2012. Methodist Theological School in Ohio library.

Keller, Rosemary Skinner, Gerald F. Moede, and Mary Elizabeth Moore. 1987. *Called to Serve: The United Methodist Diaconate.* Nashville: General Board of Higher Education and Ministry.

Lee, Daniel B. and Paul Van Buren. 1989. *Needs Assessment of Ethnic Minority Churches and Communities for Specialized Ministries,* Nashville: Division of Diaconal Ministry, General Board of Higher Education and Ministry.

Matthaei, Sondra Higgins. 2003. *The United Methodist Deacon: Servant Ministry in the Communion of the Trinity.* Occasional Papers. Nashville: General Board of Higher Education and Ministry.

Mickle, Jeffrey P., "Toward a Revised Diaconate," *Quarterly Review* 2 (1): 43–61.

Minutes of the One Hundred and Eleventh Session of the West Wisconsin Annual Conference of The United Methodist Church. June 8–11, 1965. Madison, Wisconsin.

Moede, Gerald F. 1989. *The Permanent Diaconate Revisited.* Occasional Papers No, 79. Nashville: General Board of Higher Education and Ministry.

Neville, Robert Cummings. 2002. *A Theological Analysis of the Order of Deacons in The United Methodist Church,* Occasional Papers No. 76. Nashville: General Board of Higher Education and Ministry.

Norwood, Frederick. 1960. *The Ministry in the Methodist Heritage.* Nashville: Department of Ministerial Education, The Methodist Church.

Pope Paul VI. June 18, 1967. Apostolic Letter, *General Norms for Restoring the Permanent Diaconate in the Latin Church. Sacrum Diaconatus Ordinem.* https://w2.vatican.va/content/paul–vi/en/motu_proprio/documents/hf_p–vi_motu–proprio_19670618_sacrum–diaconatus.html.

Randolph, Bonnie. "Bentzinger honored at Donnellson church," *Fort Madison Daily Democrat* (September 12, 2014). mississippivalleypublishing.com.

Rowe, Kenneth E. 1999. "The Ministry of Deacons in Methodism from Wesley to Today." *Quarterly Review* 19 (4): 343–356.

Ruch-Teegarden, Shelby. July 2019. *Women By the Numbers* "Hope for the Future and Work Yet to Finish: Deacons in The United Methodist Church." General Commission on the Status and Role of Women. https://gcsrw.org/MonitoringHistory/WomenByTheNumbers/tabid/891/post/deacons-in-The-United-Methodist-Church-2019/Default.aspx.

Study of Ministry Commission. 2020. "Report of the 2017–2020 Study of Ministry Commission Report." The United Methodist Church. https://www.gbhem.org/wp-content/uploads/2020/05/ADCA-English-Vol-2-Sec-2-SOM-c.pdf, 1005–1019.

The United Methodist Hymnal (*UMH*). 1989. Nashville: The United Methodist Publishing House.

Van Buren, Paul. *New Testament Scripture Passages,* 1993. Unpublished.

Vogel, Linda Jane. "Two Responses to 'Diaconal Ministry: Vision and Reality'" *Quarterly Review* 11 (1): 37–42.

World Council of Churches. 1982. *Baptism, Eucharist, and Ministry.* Geneva, Switzerland.

Yocom, Rena Rickman. 1991. *In Diakonia.* DMin dissertation presented to San Francisco Theological Seminary.

Notes

Prologue

1. When the deacon was approved in 1996, the *Discipline* said that deacons are ordained "to a lifetime ministry of Word and Service." ¶320. The terms *compassion* and *justice* were added by the 2012 General Conference.

2. Barnett was one of the major scholars writing about the history of *diakonia* in Christianity. His book, *The Diaconate: A Full and Equal Order,* was first published in 1981.

1. First Steps on the Path to a Renewed Diaconate

1. As early as 1934, the Methodist Episcopal Church, South had proposed standards for certifying directors of religious education that included a bachelor's degree and graduate work along with continuing education. See Furnish (1976, 150–51) for a list of the extensive qualifications.

2. This phrase is attributed to Wesley and is a favorite one for Methodists to use as their mission.

3. A copy of the service was provided to the author by the candidate whose name is now Corinne Van Buren and who is now an ordained deacon.

4. This restrictive use of the term *minister* demonstrates the understanding of the 1960s that ministry was reserved for the ordained.

2. Creating the Consecrated Diaconal Minister

1. The four calls are the call to be a Christian, the secret call, the providential call, and the ecclesiastical call. They appear in *The Purpose of the Church and Its Ministry* by H. Richard Niebuhr.

2. In 1996, there were 68 annual conferences in the US and 48 central [global] conferences; and in 2020, there were 56 annual conferences in the US and 80 central conferences.

3. Continuing to Study and Reflect

1. More areas for certification have since been added such as camping and retreat ministry, urban ministry, ministry with people with disabilities, ministry with the poor, and older adult ministry.

4. The Collective Groan in 1992

1. Use of the term *service assignments* in this report is important. The commission chose not to use the term *appointment,* which is used for the service assignment of elders, although they proposed an ordained deacon.

5. Setting the Stage

1. At that time, the courses were Old Testament, New Testament, theology, church history (including United Methodist history), mission of the Church in the world, and United Methodist doctrine and polity. Each course had to be at least two semester hours of graduate academic credit (*Book of Discipline* 1992, ¶306.3.c).

7. Perfecting, Consolidating, and Strengthening the Understanding of the Deacon

1. A fuller discussion of this issue may be found in *A Deacon's Heart: The New United Methodist Diaconate* (2001, 71–74) by Crain and Seymour. While deacons extend the eucharistic table through their service in the world, in many cases, authorization to offer the sacraments would enrich their ministry, such as a chaplain working in the crisis situations of a hospital.

2. This presentation was based on research published as *Yearning for God: Reflections of Faithful Lives* (Nashville: Upper Room Books, 2003).

3. Dr. Virginia Lee is now director of Deacon Studies at Garrett-Evangelical Theological Seminary.

8. After 25 Years, What Is a Deacon?

1. The COVID-19 pandemic has delayed the General Conference, originally scheduled for 2020, to at least 2022.

2. I am grateful for the 2020 Study of Ministry report for the terms *embodied* and *enfleshed.*

9. Already, but Not Yet

1. I use *kin-dom* because it eliminates the exclusively male aspect of the term *kingdom* and instead suggests family.

2. Wesley's Foundery Books is the publisher of this volume.

10. A Vision for the Future

1. Dr. F. Douglas Powe Jr. is director of the Lewis Center for Church Leadership and the James C. Logan Professor of Evangelism and Professor of Urban Ministry at Wesley Theological Seminary in Washington, DC.

CPSIA information can be obtained
at www.ICGtesting.com
Printed in the USA
LVHW111522300721
694156LV00006B/528

9 781953 052049